BEGINNER'S ILLUSTRATED
Guide to Gardening

Techniques to Help You Get Started

First Published in 2012 by Cool Springs Press, an imprint of the Quayside Publishing Group, 400 North First Avenue, Suite 300, Minneapolis, MN 55401 USA.

Cool Springs Press titles are also available at discounts in bulk quantity for industrial or sales-promotional use. For details write to Special Sales Manager at Cool Springs Press, 400 North First Avenue, Suite 300, Minneapolis, MN 55401 USA.

To find out more about our books, visit us online at www.coolspringspress.com.

ISBN-13: 978-1-59186-533-9

10 9 8 7 6 5 3 4 2

CIP APPLIED FOR

Project Manager: Katie Elzer-Peters
Editorial Services: Addy McCulloch and Billie Brownell
Design: Heather Claus
Principal Photography: Candace Edwards and Katie Elzer-Peters
Production Manager: Hollie Kilroy

Printed in China

BEGINNER'S ILLUSTRATED
Guide to Gardening

Techniques to Help You Get Started

Katie Elzer-Peters

COOL SPRINGS PRESS
Growing Successful Gardeners™
Minneapolis, Minnesota

Dedication

For Bob and Joy Elzer. You got me started and encouraged my love of books and gardens.

For Joseph Peters. You keep me going and never give me a hard time when I buy plants.

Acknowledgments

My sincere thanks go to Billie Brownell, who helps me see my writing anew every time we talk, and who is a tremendous source of professional support. This book would not exist without her help. I can't say enough about Heather Claus, my designer and friend, who gets in the trenches with me to help me finish all of my crazy projects. I have extreme appreciation for Candace Edwards, the principal photographer, who sweated it out with me on 95-plus degree day photo shoots during a Southern summer. I am indebted to my friends Tracy Hill, Susan Z. Miller, Jon Karschnik, Corey Creswell, Jocelyn Watson, and Jane Davis for use of their yards, modeling talents, and lawn care equipment. Creating a book is like piecing together a big puzzle, and Jenny Peterson, Addy McCulloch, Kylee Baumle, Bill Johnson, Daniel Gasteiger, Rebecca Sweet, Kathy Purdy, Lisa Grimenstein, Lee Reich, Carol Bradford, Yvonne Cunnington, Tina Koral, Mary Ann Newcomer, Barbara Wise, Jo Ellen Meyers Sharp, Dr. Michael Bradley, and many others helped me gather the pieces. Gibson's Accuprint, Pender Pines, Shelton Herb Farm, and The Coastal Roaster are three local businesses that helped greatly with logistics. There aren't enough words of thanks for my friends and family who supported me through the frantic period of producing this book. You know who you are! Though I wish I could say it to him again in person, I want to thank Roger Waynick, founder of Cool Springs Press, for believing in me and giving me the opportunity to work with him and his team. And last, but most, I could do nothing without the love and support of Joseph Peters, my husband, friend, and chief garden waterer.

—Katie Elzer-Peters

Table of Contents

Preface

I've been gardening since I could walk, so tending plants is like breathing to me. However, because I've spent my life helping people learn how to garden, I realize that's not the case for everyone. Whether you pick up this book because you've grown up watching your parents or grandparents grow beautiful flowers and you're ready to try gardening yourself, or because you have just moved into your first house with your first yard that you have to care for, I hope you find what you need to be a successful gardener.

This spring, I bought my sister Emily a garden, and we planted it together. (You can see her hand watering her plants in the "How to Care for Perennials" section.) I set out the plants and she said, "Now what? Do we just dig holes?" While working in my friend's yard (planting a garden that we photgraphed for this book), I told my friend, "You can just go to the store, buy a bunch of plants that all like sun or shade and plant them together, and they'll look good!" She said, "Well, you can do that, but I can't." I'm here to tell you that you actually *can* do that, and this book will help you learn how.

Just like cooking, painting a room, or assembling a piece of furniture, gardening requires some instructions. But while you might not hesitate to open a cookbook and whip together a new recipe you've never tried before, or begin assembling a computer desk from hundreds of parts, you might be afraid to try growing a new plant or trimming a shrub in your front yard. If so, this book is for you.

I want the information in this book to help you feel confident trying new techniques, growing new plants, and caring for your yard and garden. Plants are a lot tougher than you might think, so look up the project you want to tackle, assemble your materials, and get going. In no time, your thumb will turn green, and your yard will be the envy of your neighbors. And, if you find a plant that likes growing in your garden, buy more of it!

Happy gardening!

Katie

Introduction

Open this book to any section—"How to Prune a Tree", for example—and you'll have all of the information you need to complete a gardening technique. Each section includes a list of materials, step-by-step instructions or simple instructions for techniques that don't require multiple steps, and photographs illustrating the steps. Even if you don't know much about how to garden, you can read each section, follow the instructions, and learn how to take care of an area of your yard, lawn, or garden.

So, why an introduction?

To transform yourself from someone who mows the lawn and occasionally prunes the shrubs to a gardener with beautiful flower beds and vegetable plots, you need to learn a few basics about how to look at the landscape, where to situate plants around your house so they thrive, how plants grow, and how to find the supplies and extra information you need to be successful. Gardening is a hobby just like fly fishing or sewing— after you've learned the lingo, it is easier to read instructions, find the right supplies, and have fun while doing it. Once you've read this introduction, the information in each chapter will make more sense. You'll have a better understanding of the overall picture.

Now, let's get started!

Learning to See

How can you tell if your plants are healthy? How do you know if your garden is pretty? The first is a matter of learning how plants grow. The second is mostly a matter of personal taste. It's hard to have a pretty garden, though, if you don't understand how plants grow. That's because plants react to everything you do to them. When you fertilize, prune, or stake a plant, the plant grows a certain way. (Or stops growing, depending on what you do to it!)

A quote by Marcel Proust says, "The real voyage of discovery consists not in seeking new landscapes but in having new eyes." There are, in fact, things happening in your yard and garden right now that you might not have even noticed. Once you understand what you're looking at, you will know what to do about it. Much of gardening is in learning how to look at your plants and tell what they need: more sun, more water, more food, more shade, or a trim.

As you tend your garden using the techniques in this book, your plants will become healthier, larger, and more beautiful. You will learn to see the difference between a plant that is barely surviving and one that is thriving, and you'll know how to help the plant that's in trouble. Start learning to see by looking around your yard.

Finding Your Way Around the Yard

If you spend much time as a gardener, particularly if you start reading other gardening books and magazines, you'll frequently see the phrase "right plant, right place." You can save yourself a lot of time and money if you plant plants in areas of the garden with conditions that match growing needs listed on plant tags. For instance, select a sunny spot to plant perennials or annuals that indicate "full sun" as a growing need on their tags.

Certain types of plants are also better for some areas of the yard than others. For example, if you hear someone talking about "foundation plants," they're talking about plants next to the house—usually smaller shrubs, small trees, perennials, or annuals. An "island bed" is a landscape bed in the center of a yard, or a bed that doesn't have a driveway, sidewalk, patio, or house on one side of it.

Here's a typical yard, and the landscape features in it:

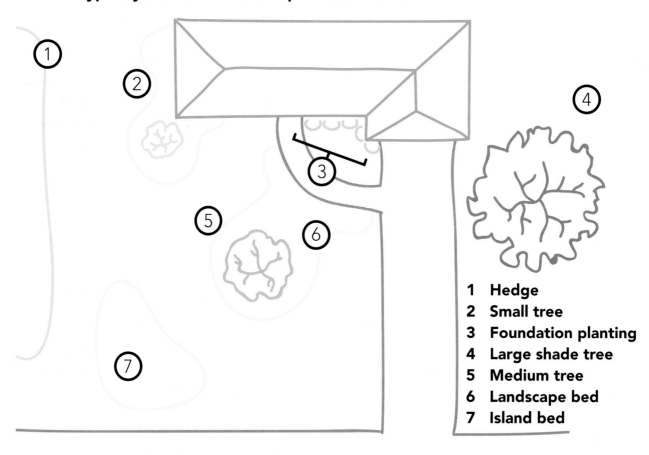

1 Hedge
2 Small tree
3 Foundation planting
4 Large shade tree
5 Medium tree
6 Landscape bed
7 Island bed

Once you know what to call different areas of the yard, it's easier to make shopping lists, because you know the types of plants to find for each area.

Going Shopping

Gardening, like other hobbies, offers tremendous opportunities to go shopping. There are thousands of different types of plants, hundreds of garden tools, and an array of fertilizers, pest control products, and mulches.

In the "What You'll Need" section right after the Introduction, you'll find pictures and descriptions of the most commonly used gardening tools and supplies, so that you can figure out what your tool shed's lacking and stock up. There's also a "What You'll Need" list for each specific technique. In "Gardening Information Decoded," you'll learn how to read seed packets, plant tags, fertilizer labels, and the USDA hardiness zone map (so that you will know how cold your area gets—important when choosing some plants). There's also information about navigating a garden center, nursery, or the garden center section of a home-improvement store. Here's some other information you need to know before shopping.

Understanding the Term "Organic"

Go shopping, open the newspaper, or look at a website, and you'll see "organic this" and "organic that" everywhere. But do you really know what *organic* means? The scientific definition of organic is an element that contains carbon. The way the word organic is used in gardening (and grocery shopping—because vegetables come from farms and gardens) is to refer to something that is made of, or grown with, naturally occurring materials. If you buy a food product labeled organic, it means that it was grown without using certain chemicals, and the grower paid the fees to be inspected for certification.

What the term organic does not mean:
- Safe
- Non-toxic

The safety of any product depends partially on how you use it. If you take a bath in pyrethrin, a natural chemical extracted from chrysanthemums, you'll get sick. You still have to take precautions when using organic materials. Remember, ricin—a highly toxic poison—is derived from the castor bean plant. It's a naturally occurring material. The best way to decide what products (fertilizers, pesticides, weed killers) to use on your lawn and garden is to read the labels and follow the instructions. The book *The Truth about Organic Gardening*, by Jeff Gillman, is one of the best sources of information about organic gardening.

Reading Tags and Labels

Spend some time reading tags and labels because they give a lot of information about where to plant things, how to use products, the type of protective gear you should wear while using a plant spray or dust, and what to do if you accidentally swallow something, get it on your skin, or splash it in your eyes. Whether something is labeled organic or natural or not, read the precautions and instructions on the label before buying it.

Asking for Help

Gardeners love talking with other gardeners, and the staff at your favorite place to buy plants will be great sources of information. If you have a problem and you need help fixing it, ask someone for more information. If you need a particular tool, ask about it! Don't be afraid to ask for help. Garden centers want you to be successful so you'll come back and shop some more, so they'll be eager to help.

Learning How Plants Grow

Once you get home, it's up to you to keep your plants growing. That's easier if you know the names of different parts of plants, and how plants grow. Here is a crash-course in botany—only the parts you need to know to be a successful gardener.

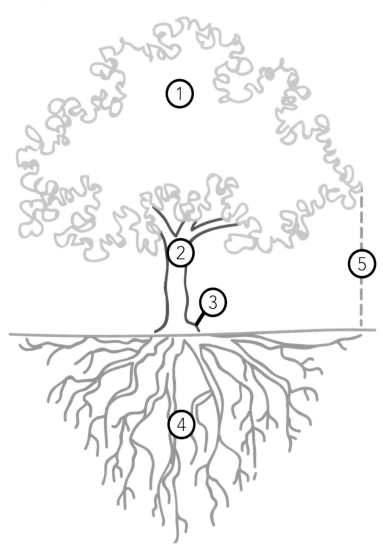

Parts of a Tree

1 Canopy

This is the top of the tree, and is made of branches and leaves.

2 Trunk

The tree's main support system, and where food and water travel up and down the tree.

3 Crown

This is the area where the trunk meets the roots. (The crown should never be under the soil or buried in mulch.)

4 Roots

These stabilize and anchor the tree, and take in water and nutrients from the soil.

5 Dripline

An imaginary line between the widest branch in the canopy and the ground below. You should water trees from the dripline in toward the trunk.

Parts of a Tree Branch

1 Branch collar

A swelling between the branch and the trunk. You always cut just outside the branch collar while pruning so the tree can heal itself.

2 Leaves

There are two parts to leaves. The petiole (2a), which is the "leaf stem" connecting the leaf to the branch, and the leaf blade (2b), which is what you think of as the leaf.

3 Buds

These are nestled between the petiole and the branch. Trees always sprout new branches from buds, which is why pruning instructions say "cut back to a leaf."

Parts of a Tree Trunk

1 Bark

The protective outer covering for the tree.

2 Xylem and phloem

The parts of the tree where food and water travel. These layers are right under the bark, so if you accidentally cut the bark all the way around the tree, the tree will starve.

3 The heartwood

This is the wood on the inside of the tree that makes up most of the trunk. This is where you see tree rings in a cross-section of a tree. This part of the tree is old growth, and is actually dead.

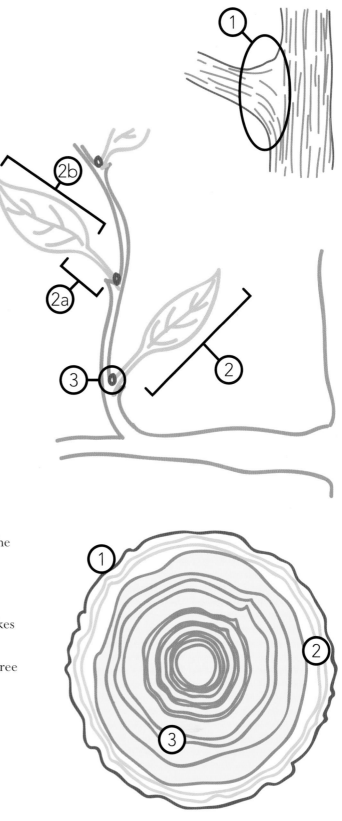

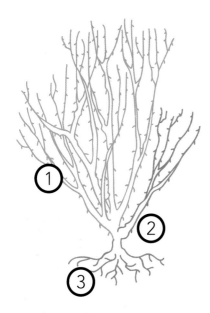

Parts of Shrubs and Roses

A shrub is like a tree without a trunk. Tree pruning techniques like cutting back to a leaf also apply to shrubs. Roses are shrubs, and they grow like other typical shrubs. Here are the parts of rose bushes and shrubs.

1   Branch (also called a "cane" on roses)

Branches make up the bulk of a shrub. Flowers and fruits form on the branches.

2   Sucker

Suckers are branches on shrubs that sprout from near the soil line, close to the roots. Many roses are actually two plants grafted together—the top is one plant and the bottom is another. A sprout coming from the roots of a rose is also called a sucker, and often looks nothing like the rest of the branches on the rose plant.

3   Roots or rootstock

The roots of all shrubs are underground. Most roses, however, are grown on what are called "rootstocks." These are roots of a hardy and tough rose variety that is more resistant to cold than most rose types. The top of a rose plant is a more sensitive flowering variety that is grafted, or joined, onto the tough rootstock.

Parts of Shrub and Rose Branches

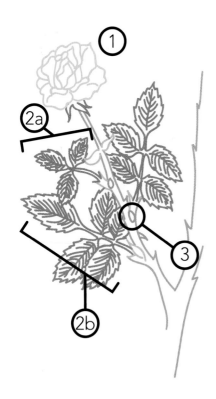

1   Flowers

Shrub flowers form along branches or at the tips of branches.

2   Leaf and leaflets

Shrubs have single or compound leaves. Roses have compound leaves with three (2a) or five (2b) leaflets. When pruning roses, you always want to cut the branch back to a leaf with five leaflets.

3   Buds

Buds are the places from which new branches sprout. They're usually nestled between the leaf petiole (bottom of the leaf) and the branch. When you prune a shrub, always cut back to one-quarter inch above a bud so that the plant will resprout and hide the cut.

Parts of a Seed

Seeds are small miracles. Inside every seed there's a baby plant and enough food to sustain that plant while it is sprouting. The seed coat protects the seed until it sprouts.

1   Embryo (baby plant)

The embryo is the baby plant inside the seed.

2   Seed leaves

Seed leaves are the first leaves that will open up after the seed sprouts.

3   Embryonic root

This part of the seed will grow to become the plant's roots.

4   Food for baby plant

Every seed has some stored food to give the plant energy to sprout and grow when conditions are right.

5   Seed coat

The outer layer of the seed.

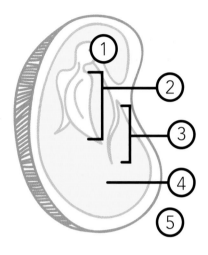

Parts of a Sprouting Seed

1   First true leaves

The first set of leaves that the plant grows after it sprouts. (They are above the seed leaves.)

2   Seed leaves

These are the first leaves that you see after a seed sprouts. They were the leaves stored inside the seed. Seed leaves usually look a little bit different from the true leaves. They're smaller, rounder, and lighter in color.

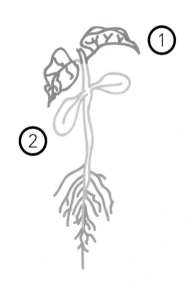

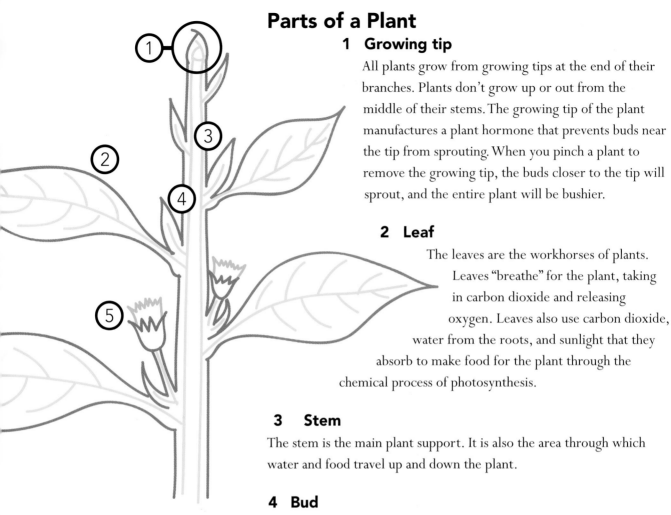

Parts of a Plant

1 Growing tip

All plants grow from growing tips at the end of their branches. Plants don't grow up or out from the middle of their stems. The growing tip of the plant manufactures a plant hormone that prevents buds near the tip from sprouting. When you pinch a plant to remove the growing tip, the buds closer to the tip will sprout, and the entire plant will be bushier.

2 Leaf

The leaves are the workhorses of plants. Leaves "breathe" for the plant, taking in carbon dioxide and releasing oxygen. Leaves also use carbon dioxide, water from the roots, and sunlight that they absorb to make food for the plant through the chemical process of photosynthesis.

3 Stem

The stem is the main plant support. It is also the area through which water and food travel up and down the plant.

4 Bud

The bud is a new plant branch and growing tip waiting to sprout. The buds are nestled between a leaf and a branch or stem.

5 Flower

Flowers are the reproductive parts of plants. In order to to fruit or produce seeds, the plant flowers must be pollinated by insects, birds, or wind.

Parts of a Flower

Flowers are the plant's reproductive system. It's important to know that, because to trick the plant into continuing to bloom, you will cut off the faded flowers to prevent plants from setting seeds.

1 Stamen

Stamens are the male parts of a plant. They produce pollen.

2 Pistil

The female part of a plant is called the pistil. Pollen lands on the sticky top of a pistil to fertilize a plant.

3 Petal

Petals attract pollinators to fertilize a plant.

4 Ovary

The ovary is at the bottom of a pistil. Once a plant is pollinated, the ovary matures into a seed or fruit.

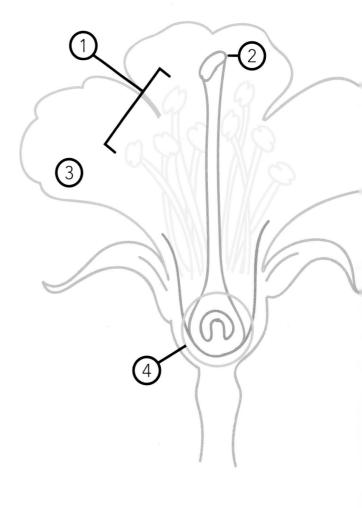

Plant seeds are parts of the fruits

Did you know that anything you eat that has seeds is actually a fruit even if you call it a vegetable? Peppers, eggplants, and tomatoes are all fruits. If someone describes a tomato plant as "fruiting," they're saying that there are tomatoes ripening on the plant.

Seeds inside a tomato

Seeds form inside the fruit of a plant. There are different kinds of fruits. Maple tree fruits look like helicopters and they don't have squishy flesh around the seeds like tomatoes do. Maple trees rely on wind to carry their seeds far away. Tomato plants, apple trees, and other plants with delicious edible fruits rely on animals to disperse their seeds.

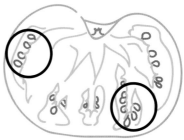

Growing as a Gardener

Practice makes perfect, especially with gardening. Just like the first soufflé you make might not be the fluffiest, or the first fly you tie might not be as precise, your first attempts at gardening could produce interesting results. Here's a little secret though: even experienced gardeners kill plants, prune things the wrong way, or end up needing to move a plant because it outgrew its space. Following good gardening instructions (like those in this book) will help you be more successful, but you'll always learn some things by trial and error.

Looking for Information

When you're first starting out, it's important to get correct information. If you search the Internet for gardening information, search for sites with .edu at the end of the Internet address. This will help you find information from university Extension offices and horticulture departments, written by people with professional training and experience.

The important thing is to keep growing—literally and figuratively. Keep learning new information, trying new techniques, and growing new plants.

What You'll Need

Tools

Rarely will you meet a seasoned gardener who doesn't enjoy trying out a new tool. *Everybody* has his own personal preference about the tool he can't live without—pruners that fit his hand just so, or the hoe that makes light work of planting and weeding. Once you've gardened for a while, you'll have your favorite too. And then the tool manufacturers will come up with something new for you to try.

There are some tools that every gardener needs. You'll want to stock your tool shed with both a shovel (which has a long, straight handle) and a spade (which has a short handle with a grip on the end). The following pages show you which tools you'll need to care for your plants.

Supplies

In addition to long-lasting tools, gardening requires supplies that are used up from year to year. Potting soil, seed starting mix, mulch—there are many choices for each type of garden supply needed to keep plants healthy. This section shows you how to choose the essentials you'll need to get started.

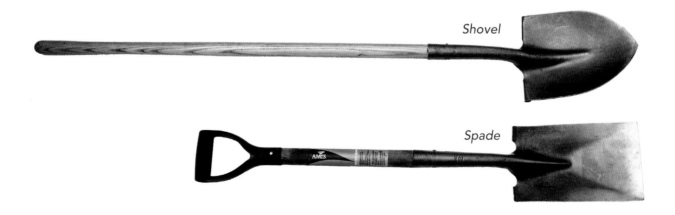

Shovel

Spade

Pruning and Staking Tools

Pruning and staking tools help you do a few things in the garden.

- Remove dead or diseased plant parts
- Control plant size (width and height)
- Control plant shape (round, square, growing up, or spreading out)

Pruning Tools

Snips

Snips are a cross between scissors and hand pruners. They have a scissor-like cutting action, but they have a spring like hand pruners, for easy cutting. Snips are great for deadheading.

Scissors

A good pair of scissors is a must for the garden. Use them to snip twine, deadhead, and cut flowers.

Hand pruners

Hand pruners have a cutting blade and an anchor blade. They're good for pruning, deadheading, and cutting bamboo stakes.

Pruning saw

Pruning saws fold up for easy toting in the garden basket. They are handy for cutting branches over 2 inches in diameter.

Hedge trimmers

Hedge trimmers have long, flat blades to cut large areas of shrubs to the same length at once. You can also get electric hedge trimmers. When using those, always watch the cord so you don't cut it in half!

Loppers

Loppers are like big hand pruners. They have the same type of cutting blade, but usually it is larger. Loppers also have longer handles. They're good for trimming shrubs and tree branches that are out of arm's reach.

Snips

Scissors

Hand pruners

Pruning saw

Hedge trimmers

Loppers

Velcro

Twine

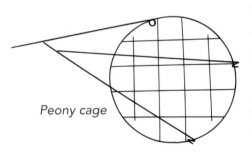

Wire

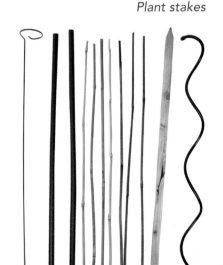

Peony cage

Plant stakes

Staking Tools

Velcro, twine, wire

You always need something to tie a plant to a stake. Velcro and wire can be re-used and work well with vegetables. Twine is invaluable to have on hand because it is versatile. You can use it to stake larger groups of plants and create webs for plants to grow through. Jute twine (pictured) is the most commonly used type of garden twine because it is strong.

Peony cage

These plant supports are good for any clumping perennial with skinny stems and big flowers that tends to flop. The cage is a ring of metal with an interior grid. The ring is on three or four legs. You push the legs into the soil when the plants are first sprouting so that they can grow up through the grid support.

Plant stakes

You can use anything long and narrow to stake plants. When you buy stakes, you'll run into a few common types. Here's more about each of the stakes pictured bottom, left, from left to right.

Single-stem metal stake

These stakes are good for plants with tall, vertical flowers. Orchids, delphinium, and larkspur grow well with these supports that have a circle and hook on one end.

Metal or plastic-coated metal stake

These heavy-duty stakes are perfect for vegetable gardening. They won't break as plants get tall and heavy.

Natural and dyed bamboo stakes and wood stakes

The light color of natural bamboo stakes and wood stakes makes them stand out more against dark green garden foliage, while the dyed green stakes blend in. All are easy to cut to size with hand pruners.

Tomato spiral

For use with tomatoes, which can twine around the sprial for support.

Trellis

There are trellises made of wood and trellises made of metal. Some trellises are wire and hook assemblies that you create on a wall or fence. Use a trellis to support vines, climbing vegetables, and large, floppy plants.

Tomato cage

Tomato cages are made of aluminum and provide support for tomatoes, peppers, eggplants, tomatillos, and any large vegetables.

Digging, Raking, and Spreading Tools

Use these tools when planting, weeding, mulching, cleaning up the garden, and planting plants.

Digging Tools

Pickahoe

The scary-looking pickahoe actually makes planting easier and faster. This is a hoe with a sharp blade and a short handle. Use it as you would use a pickaxe to quickly dig holes for planting annuals or bulbs.

Trowel

Trowels are small shovels used for weeding and planting. You can buy trowels made of plastic or made with metal blades and wood handles.

Soil knife

Soil knives are indispensable. One side of the blade is sharpened, and the other is serrated like a saw. Use these to plant bulbs, dig up weeds, and cut through roots. Some soil knives have depth measurements marked on them, which help with planting.

Hand weeder

Hand weeders are tools with thin metal blades good for cutting out, digging up, or turning over weeds.

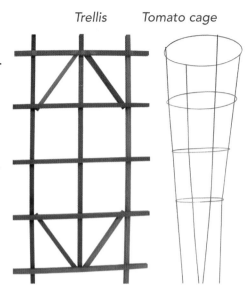

Trellis   *Tomato cage*

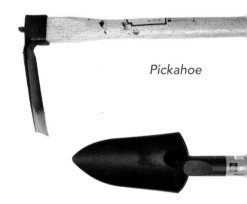

Pickahoe

Trowel

Soil knife

Hand weeder

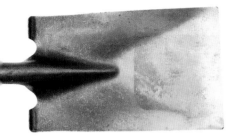

Spade

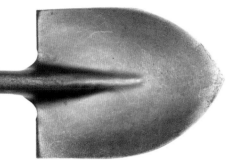

Shovel

Hoe

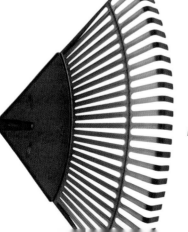

Shrub rake

Spade

Spades are shovels that have short handles with grips that you can put your hand through on the end, as opposed to a straight handle without a grip like most shovels. (A spade handle is usually 2 to 3 feet shorter than a shovel handle.) Most spades have square heads with flat bottoms (like the one pictured). Use spades to edge landscape beds or dig trenches. You can sharpen the metal ends of spades to make it easier to dig and cut through the soil.

Shovel

Shovels have long, straight wood handles and curved or straight bottoms. Use shovels to dig up plants, dig planting holes for trees and shrubs, and to plant gallon-sized perennials.

Hoe

There are many different types of hoes. Hoes with narrow ends are excellent for digging planting rows. Hoes with larger, wider ends are helpful for spreading soil and mulching.

Raking and Spreading Tools

Shrub rake

Shrub rakes are among the handiest garden tools available. They usually have small plastic heads that are about one-third to one-fourth as wide as leaf rakes, and their tines are made of plastic. Use shrub rakes to spread mulch between perennial plants, to remove trash from under shrubs, and to remove leaves or snow from the tops of shrubs.

Leaf rake

You can buy metal or plastic leaf rakes. Leaf rakes have long handles and large, somewhat flat raking heads with curved tines on the end. Use leaf rakes to rake leaves, clean out garden and landscape beds in the spring, and rake grass clippings. Leaf rakes with plastic tines tend to be softer and damage plants less than leaf rakes with metal tines, if you rake over your plants.

Leaf rake

4 tine claw

A 4 tine claw has a long wood handle and metal top with four curved tines. (This tool is sometimes called a cultivator.) Use a 4 tine claw to cultivate and dig between vegetable garden rows, rake mulch in narrow garden beds, and to incorporate compost and soil amendments into the garden.

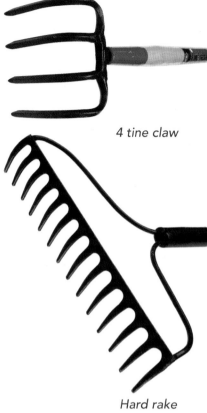

4 tine claw

Hard rake

A hard rake is a cross between a leaf rake and a 4 tine claw. It has hard metal prongs like a claw, but a wider head like a leaf rake. Use this to rake soil and spread mulch. Hard rakes are also useful for spreading gravel and raking mulch pathways.

Garden fork and pitchfork

Pitchforks have long, straight handles and scooped heads similar to shovels, but they have sharpened tines instead of solid metal blades. Use pitchforks to turn the compost pile and move mulch around. Garden forks have handles like spades—with a grip you can put your hand through on the end—but they have flat tines that are wider than pitchfork tines. Use garden forks to divide plants and turn over weeds.

Hard rake

Shop broom

Shop brooms are large push brooms that come in handy for cleaning sidewalks and driveways. Hose off the shop broom every now and then to clean it.

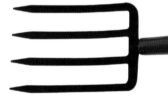

Garden fork

Success Tip

Keep your tools inside when you're not using them. If wood handles get wet, they can swell and crack. Plastic tools degrade if left out in the sun and will weaken and eventually crack. Metal tines can rust. Get a tool rack especially for holding your garden tools and always take the time to put them up when you're done. Five minutes at the end of a job saves money and time later.

Shop broom

Garden hose

Soaker hose

Sprinkler

Watering Tools

Garden hose

The garden hose is your main tool for watering plants. It's worth the money to buy a good 50-foot, heavy-duty, no-kink hose. You'll be glad you made the extra investment.

Soaker hose

Soaker hoses are porous hoses that you connect to a faucet, place, and leave in the garden. When you turn on the faucet, water slowly seeps out of the hose, reaching the plants where they need it most—their roots. Use soaker hoses if you don't have the time or money to create drip irrigation systems. Soaker hoses come in handy during short hot and dry periods because they're easy to move around. You can also get sprinkler timers to put on the ends of soaker hoses to create your own DIY irrigation system that will turn on and off while you're out of town.

Sprinkler

Sprinklers attach to the ends of hoses and disperse the water over wide areas. There are rotating sprinklers and impact sprinklers. Use sprinklers to water the lawn. If you don't have soaker hoses or enough time to water the vegetables, you can use sprinklers in the vegetable garden, too, but overhead watering (watering from above) can spread diseases. (Fungi and bacteria spores travel quickly through water.)

Hose guide

If you have to wind your hose around lots of flower beds, hose guides will become your best friend. Put these in the ground at flower bed corners to keep the hose out of the garden beds. You can find decorative hose guides that act as garden ornaments. Some hose guides have rings through which you'll thread the hose to keep it in place. The green hose guide pictured has a rotating top which makes it slightly easier to pull the hose through the guide.

Hose guide

Watering wand

Watering wand

Every gardener needs a watering wand. This is a long tube with a water breaker on the end that disperses the water pressure from the hose. Watering wands make it easy for you to water near the base of a plant without bending over, or to reach up and water hanging baskets.

Spray nozzle

Don't use spray nozzles to water plants. Use these nozzles, which actually *increase* the pressure of the water flow, to blast insects off of flower and vegetable plants.

Spray nozzle

Flower pot and saucer

Always use plant saucers under containers to collect water runoff. Plants will soak up the water as the soil in the pot dries. On hot, dry days, fill the saucer with water so that plants have it available during the day.

Flower pot and saucer

Watering can

Watering cans make quick work of watering containers and flower pots without watering everything else around them. Keep a watering can handy next to each hose. Fill watering cans from rain barrels to easily use rain barrel water too. Houseplant watering cans have narrower spouts than watering cans used outside.

Success Tip

Always store your watering tools inside for the winter, particularly nozzles, wands, and breakers. If you leave them outside when you're not using them, they'll rust, and will be ruined in one season. Take good care of them and they'll last longer. During the growing season, it is nice to stash a water breaker or watering wand near every hose so you don't have to move your tools around so much.

Watering can

Water breaker

Organic liquid fertilizer

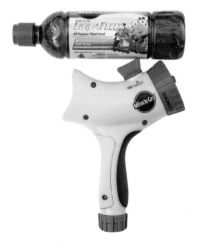

Liquid fertilizer

Water breaker

Water breakers can be used with watering wands or on the ends of hoses. Sometimes called rosettes, water breakers disperse the flow of water so that it is softer and less likely to cause soil to splatter. Water breakers should be used when you're hand-watering plants. They're especially good for watering newly planted plants.

Fertilizer, Soil, and Mulch

Fertilizer

Liquid organic or natural fertilizer

Organic or natural fertilizers are usually made from kelp, fish emulsion, or a combination of each. Mix this type of fertilizer with water in watering cans to water into the soil. Some liquid organic or natural fertilizers are used as foliar feeds. Mix these fertilizers with water in a pressurized sprayer and spray the leaves of the plants. The plants will soak up the nutrients through their leaves. Organic fertilizers are smelly, so don't use them right before you have an outdoor barbecue.

Liquid conventional or synthetic fertilizer

Synthetic fertilizers have Nitrogen, Phosphorous, and Potassium in them in one combination or another. These fertilizers are formulated for different types of plants. You can buy houseplant fertilizers, fertilizers for acid-loving plants, vegetable fertilizers, and fertilizers formulated to encourage more blooms on plants. You can buy conventional fertilizer in concentrated liquid forms (pictured) and concentrated powder forms. In both cases, you need to mix the concentrate with water. Some brands of fertilizer have special attachments that will do the mixing for you (pictured).

Granular fertilizer

Granular or slow-release fertilizer feeds plants over a period of three to five months. The nutrients in the fertilizer are pelletized in a form that breaks down and releases nutrients to plants over time. Sometimes granular fertilizer is combined with pre-emergent weed control in a "weed and feed" product. Don't use weed and feed products where you've just planted seeds, or they won't sprout.

Blood meal and plant tone

Blood meal, bone meal, and plant tones are organic slow-release fertilizers. They're made from animal products and are sprinkled around the plants (this is called side dressing) and worked into the soil with a 4 tine claw. Just like synthetic fertilizers, you can buy plant tones for acid-loving plants, vegetables, flowers, and trees. Each type has different combinations of nutrients and ingredients to best benefit the receiving plants. These fertilizers are also smelly, so apply them a few days before you plan to spend time in the yard so you don't have to smell them.

Worm castings and soil conditioner

Worm castings (worm poop) are expensive to buy, but they're wonderful for garden plants, particularly vegetables. Worm castings and soil conditioner are similar products, in that they are both almost entirely composed of humic acid, which is the most decomposed element in soil. Humic acid is excellent for plants. Incorporate worm castings or soil conditioner into your soil before planting, and you'll be amazed at how well your plants grow.

You can make your own worm castings by becoming a worm farmer. Buy a worm bin and follow the directions for procuring worms and feeding the worms. Worm composting is a great way to get rid of kitchen scraps.

Granular fertilizer

Plant tone

Worm castings

Seed starting mix

Potting mix

Garden soil

Compost

Soil

Seed starting mix

Seed starting mix is actually not soil; it is a lightweight soilless mix made from peat moss, perlite, and other ingredients. It is perfect for starting seeds. Seed starting mix is usually sterilized to prevent diseases that live in the soil from harming seedlings. It really does make a difference if you use seedling mix to start seeds—both indoors and out.

Potting mix

Potting mix is specially formulated to use in containers. In addition to soil, potting mix usually has perlite to help keep the soil moist, and sometimes has water-holding crystals so that you can water plants less frequently. When planting container gardens, always use potting soil. Some potting soils have slow-release fertilizer in them to make it easier and less time consuming to feed plants.

Garden soil and topsoil

Garden soil and topsoil are coarser soils that you can use to build up areas of the garden where soil has washed away. Some bagged garden soil has slow-release fertilizer mixed into it. Generally, it's helpful to mix garden soil or topsoil with compost before planting a garden bed. The compost adds nutrients and natural water-holding components.

Compost and manure

You can make your own compost, but you can also buy compost and composted manure. Cow, rabbit, chicken, and mushroom compost are the most commonly available types. Manure and compost improve soil structure, which makes it easier for plants to grow. These soil amendments also have nutrients that benefit plants and components that help water stay in the soil and available to plants. If you get manure from a local farm, make sure that it has been sitting and aging for at least six months. Ammonia in fresh manure can burn your plants. Never use cat or dog droppings in the garden.

Mulch

Bark mulch

Most people mulch their gardens with bark and wood mulch. Pine bark nuggets, shredded hardwood bark, and shredded cedar bark mulch are the most common types of wood mulch. You can buy wood mulch in bags by the cubic foot or in bulk. Bulk mulch is loose (not in bags) and can be picked up with a truck or delivered. If you're going to need more than 3 cubic yards of mulch, it is a good idea to look into delivery.

Bark mulch

Gravel mulch

If you live in a desert or dry climate, try mulching with rocks. You can buy bagged or bulk river rocks, marble chips, and pea gravel. Before putting rocks in the landscape bed, first lay down a layer of weed cloth. Weed cloth is a porous fabric that lets water pass through but keeps weeds from sprouting. For good measure, spread pre-emergent herbicide on top of the weed cloth. Then spread the rocks or gravel.

Gravel mulch

Straw

Pine straw mulch is common in the South, where long-needled pine trees grow. This mulch is sold in bales. You use the rake-and-tuck technique to spread pine straw and put finishing touches on the landscape bed. This technique is explained in the mulching chapter.

Wheat straw is useful for vegetable beds, and is available at most garden centers or home-improvement stores.

Success Tip

When selecting mulch for your garden, choose a material that goes well with the rest of your garden and house. For example, if you live in the woods, white marble rock chips will look unnatural and strange. Go for straw or shredded hardwood instead. Pine straw looks good in beds around large pine trees, but strange at the beach. Red volcanic rock looks fine in desert gardens, but weird in Midwestern gardens.

Pine straw mulch

Weed and Pest Control Tools

Equipment

Gloves and dust mask

Regardless of whether you're spreading or spraying organic or conventional pesticides, always wear nitrile gloves. These gloves are specially made to withstand chemicals. When using dust or powdered pesticides, wear a dust mask or respirator. For exact instructions on the specific type of protective gear that you should wear while applying a specific product, always read the label on the product.

Safety glasses

Safety glasses

Safety glasses are handy for pruning (so you don't get poked in the eye), and they're also a must when applying pest control products so that you don't splash or blow the products into your eyes.

Pressure sprayer

Pressure sprayer

There are hand sprayers, backpack sprayers, and sprayers on wheels. You build up pressure by pumping a handle on the top or side.

Rotary spreader

Spread grass seed, fertilizer, and weed control products on your lawn with a rotary spreader.

Rotary spreader

Weed and Pest Control Products

Insecticidal soap

Insecticidal soap is a specially formulated insecticide that kills soft bodied insects such as aphids by drying them out. It is better to use this in your garden than dish soap from your kitchen, because insecticidal soap is mixed specifically for use on plants.

Insecticidal soap

Repellent spray

Repellent sprays are mixtures of essential oils that pests like deer, rabbits, and mosquitos don't like to smell or taste. Spray these every three months in the garden to keep pests from eating your plants. Every six months, switch the brand of repellent you're using because pests eventually become accustomed to the scents and will no longer be repelled by them.

Repellent spray

Horticultural oil

Horticultural oil used to be called dormant oil because you would spray plants only when they were dormant (and had no leaves). Most horticultural oils can be sprayed at any time, as long as the temperatures are below 75 degrees. These pesticides work by clogging the pores and breathing orifices of insects and suffocating them. If sprayed at the wrong time, they can also clog the pores on leaves and suffocate the plant. Because they're oil products, if they're sprayed when it is hot, they will, literally, fry the plant leaves!

Horticultural oil

Diatomaceous earth

Diatomacous earth acts as a pest control barrier. It is a fine powder made from crushed, fossilized sea creatures. Slugs and snails don't like the rough surface that diatomaceous creates, and won't crawl across it.

Diatomaceous earth

Fungicide

Weed killer

Pre-emergent herbicide

Broadleaf weed killer

Fungicide

There are many kinds of fungicides. This picture shows a rose care product with fungicide to get rid of blackspot. Before spraying a fungicide, make sure you have correctly identified the fungus you're spraying for, and buy the right product to use. Always read the instructions on the label before using a fungicide.

Insecticide

There is an insecticide to kill almost every pest. (Insecticidal soap is a natural insecticide.) They come in sprays, powders, and granules. Some kill on contact (when they hit the pest) and some are systemic, which means that the pest has to absorb or ingest the product (usually by eating the plant that you've sprayed with insecticide) in order to die. Always identify the pest you want to kill and purchase a product labeled to kill that pest. Always read and follow instructions on the label.

Broad-spectrum weed killer

Some weed killers are selective, meaning they kill broad leaves (like dandelions) or grasslike weeds. Other weed killers kill *all* plants. Read the label to make sure you're buying the type of weed killer you need. If you spray a broad-spectrum weed killer on the grass, you'll kill the weeds and the grass too.

Pre-emergent herbicide

Pre-emergent herbicide prevents seeds (including weed seeds) from sprouting. It doesn't work on weeds that are already growing. Use corn gluten as an organic pre-emergent herbicide. Weed and feed products have fertilizer and pre-emergent herbicide in them. Pre-emergent herbicide works for 3 to 6 months and then has to be re-applied.

Broadleaf weed killer

This weed killer kills broadleaf weeds but leaves grass and grasslike plants alone. If you have a weedy lawn, broadleaf weed killer can help. Never use weed killers when the temperature is above 80 degrees Fahrenheit.

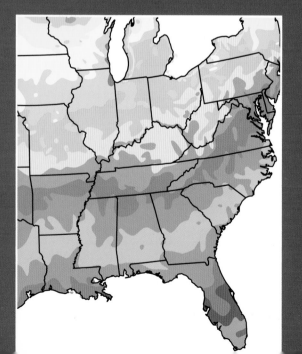

Part One: Gardening Information Decoded

What You'll Learn

Gardening has its own language and information, just like any other hobby or activity. If you've never been taught how to read the labels on gardening supplies, plants, or seeds, everything gets confusing, fast. How do you know if you're buying enough seeds? How do you know if the tree you're looking at in the garden center or home-improvement store is going to perfectly fit or outgrow your yard?

There's lots of useful information on plant tags and product labels—if you know how to read them. In this part, you'll learn how to read and understand these labels so that you can select the right plants and products for your gardening projects.

Know the Lingo

Look up the definitions of these terms in the glossary before reading through this part, and you'll have a leg up on your learning!

- Annual
- Common name
- Deciduous plant
- Dormant
- Evergreen
- Four-inch pot
- Full sun
- Gallon container
- Mulch
- Organic
- Perennial
- Scientific name
- Shrub
- Tree
- Vegetable

How to Navigate a Garden Center

One of the most fun parts of gardening is shopping. One of the most intimidating parts for a new gardener is shopping and finding the supplies you need. Whether you shop at a mom-and-pop store or a large home-improvement store, you will find roughly the same types of supplies in approximately the same groupings. Here's how to navigate a standalone garden center or a large home-improvement store garden center, inside and out.

Outside at the Garden Center

Seasonal Highlights

To lure you in, garden centers put their prettiest, most colorful plants right up front. In the springtime, you'll find pansies and violas, alyssum and petunias. During the summer, orange and yellow marigolds, fire-engine red salvia, and bright white periwinkle will be on display. In the fall, huge pots of burgundy, orange, yellow, and pink chrysanthemums beckon you to shop. So, if you want something that says "celebrate the season," check the front of the store.

Annuals and Perennials

Most garden centers put their annuals and perennials close to the front because they're also colorful plants. Some places will display all of one kind of plant together—all of the different colors of marigolds, all of the petunias, all of the hostas—while others will create themed displays, like butterfly or bird gardens. Every garden center will group sun annuals together, sun perennials together, shade annuals together, and shade perennials together. They don't always separate plants by water needs, so read the tags!

Trees and Shrubs

Generally, you'll find trees and shrubs at the back of the store, though if trees are blooming, sometimes there will be a few at the front. Evergreen trees (trees that keep their leaves all year) will be grouped together, and deciduous trees (trees that lose their leaves in the winter) will be grouped together. Fruit trees will have their own section. Shrubs are sometimes lumped together, so check the tags if you are looking for deciduous or evergreen, sun or shade.

Bulk Materials

Larger garden centers and home-improvement stores will sell some bulk materials. Mulch, topsoil, rocks, steppingstones, and bricks are the most common bulk materials you'll find. Some stores sell these by the piece, others by the weight—it depends on the store and the material. Always ask for help with bulk materials.

Bagged Goods

Bagged goods will be inside or outside, depending on the product. Grass seed, fertilizer, and soil amendments like lime are sold by weight, and are usually inside. Mulch and soil are sold by the cubic foot (usually in 2- or 4-cubic-foot-sized bags) and are usually stored outside.

Containers

Large pottery containers will usually be stacked up outside. Plastic containers and houseplant containers might be inside. There are thousands of container choices, but always look for containers with drainage holes in them. Otherwise, you'll have to plant a pot within a pot so that the plants don't get too soggy.

Inside at the Garden Center

Tools

Look inside (or at least under cover) for watering tools, pruners, shovels and rakes, and replacement parts. Home-improvement stores sell shovels and their wood replacement handles. Ask for help if you need replacement parts. Lawn mowers, string trimmers, and power tools are always inside, as are their replacement parts and oil.

Fertilizer and Pest Control

Sometimes fertilizer products and pest control products (weed killer, insect killer) are in the same aisle, and sometimes they're in different aisles. Sometimes organic or natural remedies are shelved together with conventional remedies; sometimes they're separated. When shopping for fertilizer or pest control, always carefully read the labels on products so that you know that what you're buying is what you need to feed the plant, kill the insect, or kill the weed.

Indoor Plants

The indoor plant section is often in a small conservatory or greenhouse somewhere in the garden center or home-improvement store. Sometimes the sign says "tropical plants." Other times it says "foliage" or "houseplants." Look for houseplant supplies in the same area, including fertilizer, African violet fertilizer, houseplant pots, stakes, and seed-starting supplies.

Know the Lingo

Before you can go home and get in the garden, you need to assemble the right materials. Here's how to understand what garden center signs say, and what they mean to you as a gardener.

What the Sign Says	What the Sign Means
$12 per flat	Price for the entire flat.
$5 per six-pack	Price per cell-pack with six plants in it.
Annuals	Plants that grow for one year or one season.
Bagged goods	Mulch, soil, potting soil that is sold in bags.
Bedding plants	Annual flowers sold in flats.
Bulk materials	Mulch, soil, potting soil, gravel that is sold by weight from big piles.
Drought-tolerant	Plants that don't need extra water once they've been in the garden for a year.
Edibles	Vegetable, herb, and fruit plants.
Evergreens	Plants that keep their leaves all year.
Groundcovers	Short plants that grow fast—to plant in place of a lawn.
Hanging baskets	Plants planted in baskets with hooks for hanging.
Hardy	Plant that will survive the winter in your area.
Native plants	Usually means a plant that naturally grows in the surrounding area, or North America.
Nursery	Can refer to area of the store with plants, or area of the store with trees.
Perennials	Plants that come back year after year.
Pottery	Usually means ceramic flower pots, fountains, or statues.
Remedies	Sometimes used to refer to organic or natural pest control products.
Seasonal color	Annual or perennial flowers that bloom during a specific season, such as mums in the fall.
Shade plants	Plants that need full shade, or no more than early morning sun.
Sun plants	Plants that need at least 6 to 8 hours of sunlight per day.
Tropicals	Houseplants or larger potted plants that you bring inside in the winter, such as hibiscus.
Vegetables	Vegetable transplants, sets, starts, or bulbs.

How to Read a Plant Tag

When you go to the garden center or home-improvement store to buy plants, make sure to check the plant tags—they're filled with information. You'll find that, while each brand of plant has a different style of tag, they all have the same types of information. Here's how to decode the labels on the plants you're buying to make sure you buy the right plant for the right place.

1 Common name

This is the common name of the plant. This name can change from region to region, as the common name is usually influenced by local history. The same plant could be called "ironweed," "bug snatcher," or "squirrel weed" in different areas of the country.

2 Scientific name

This two-part (or sometimes three-part) name is the plant's scientific name, which is written in botanical Latin and is standard throughout the world. The first word is the genus. The second word is the species.

3 Plant type

You'll buy plants in these common categories: bulbs, annuals, perennials, vegetables, trees, shrubs, vines, tropicals, or groundcovers.

PRETTY FLOWER
Plantus prettyus

LIGHT	PLANT SPACING	MATURE HEIGHT	WATER NEEDS
Partial Sun	2 in.	12-18 in.	Medium

Blooms: Mid-Spring

Plant Apr - Jul
Plant Mar - Aug
Plant Feb - Jul
Plant Jan - Jun
Plant Sep - Mar

Pretty Flower is an easy-to-grow perennial that grows well in partial shade, medium moist soil, and is hardy in zones 4-9. Butterflies love to visit this plant for nectar.

4 Light requirements

Every plant has specific light requirements. Some prefer full sun (6 to 8 hours per day), while others need full shade. Always select plants with light requirements that match the areas where you will be planting them.

5 Spacing between plants

You'll usually buy perennials in four-inch pots or in gallon containers. These plants will grow, doubling or even tripling in size over a period of a few years. Pay attention to the spacing indications on the plant tags, because this indicates the mature spread and size of the plant. It's easy to plant a lot of things close together for a finished look, but you'll spend a lot of time dividing and moving plants around if you ignore plant spacing needs.

6 Mature height

This measurement indicates the height of the plant while it is in bloom. On tree and shrub tags, the height measurement indicates the mature height of the tree or shrub, which could take as many as forty years to reach.

7 Water requirements

As important as light requirements are water requirements. Some plants like the soil to dry out before you water them again. Others don't mind or even thrive in soil that stays moist all of the time. Always group plants together that need the same amount of water.

How to Read a Seed Packet

When you head to the garden center or home-improvement store to pick out seeds for your garden, you'll be more likely to select the right seeds to grow if you understand the information on the seed packet. Different brands of seeds have slightly different seed packet designs, but they all have roughly the same information. Vegetable seed packets have additional information about harvesting. Here's how to read seed packets.

Flower Seed Packet

1 **Common name**
2 **Scientific name**
3 **Plant type**

Annual flowers complete their entire life cycle during one growing season. They sprout, bloom, and die in one year. They do not come back from year to year from their roots, as perennials do.

4   Weight of seeds in packet

Seeds are packed by weight, not volume. Often, the weight is accompanied by information about how much space you can plant with the seeds contained in the packet.

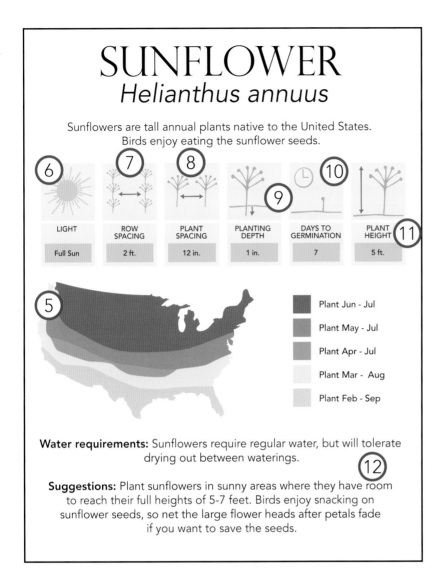

SUNFLOWER
Helianthus annuus

Sunflowers are tall annual plants native to the United States.
Birds enjoy eating the sunflower seeds.

LIGHT	ROW SPACING	PLANT SPACING	PLANTING DEPTH	DAYS TO GERMINATION	PLANT HEIGHT
Full Sun	2 ft.	12 in.	1 in.	7	5 ft.

Plant Jun - Jul

Plant May - Jul

Plant Apr - Jul

Plant Mar - Aug

Plant Feb - Sep

Water requirements: Sunflowers require regular water, but will tolerate drying out between waterings.

Suggestions: Plant sunflowers in sunny areas where they have room to reach their full heights of 5-7 feet. Birds enjoy snacking on sunflower seeds, so net the large flower heads after petals fade if you want to save the seeds.

5   When to plant

Most seed packets have information about when to plant. Some packets will tell you how warm the soil needs to be for seeds to sprout, but most packets have zone maps that allow you to locate your approximate zone to see when's the best time to plant outside. (Zone maps tell you when to plant outside—not when to start seeds inside.)

6   Light requirements

Most annual flowers grow best in the sun, though there are a few shade-lovers. Always match the light requirement on the seed packet with the conditions in the location where you plan to plant the seeds.

7   Row spacing

The amount of space you need to leave between rows of seeds.

8   Plant spacing

How far apart to plant the seeds.

9   Planting depth

How deep to plant the seeds.

10 Days to germination

How many days it will take for the seed to sprout after planting. In general, plants germinate faster when temperatures are higher and slower when temperatures are lower.

11 Plant height

The height of the fully grown plant. You don't necessarily need to plant tall plants in the back of the bed and short plants in the front, but you will want to look for plants that have different heights so that every plant in the flower bed isn't the same height. Staggering the heights makes it easier to actually see your flowers and plants.

12 Water requirements and suggestions

Every plant has different water requirements. Always plant things with similar water needs next to one another.

Vegetable Seed Packet

Vegetable seed packets have information that isn't usually on flower seed packets. This information indicates whether something is a hybrid or heirloom variety. There's always information about "days to maturity" after planting, which indicates the number of days between planting the seeds and harvesting vegetables. Seed packets will also indicate whether a plant is resistant to certain diseases.

1 Common name
2 Scientific name
3 Type of plant

Hybrids are created from two plants that have been bred. You cannot plant the seeds from hybrids and grow a plant that is the same as the parent plant.

4 Weight

Seed packets are packed by weight, not by volume. The same number of tomato seeds and bean seeds take up very different amounts of space and have different weights.

5 "Packed for" date

All seeds must be sold to customers before the end of the "packed for" year.

6 When to plant outside

Look at the zone map on the back of the seed packet to determine when you can sow seeds or plant transplants outside in your area. The outdoor planting date is the same whether you're planting seeds or transplants.

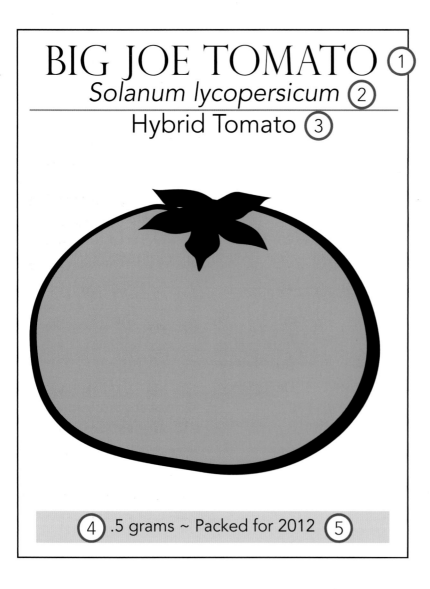

BIG JOE TOMATO ①
Solanum lycopersicum ②
Hybrid Tomato ③

④ .5 grams ~ Packed for 2012 ⑤

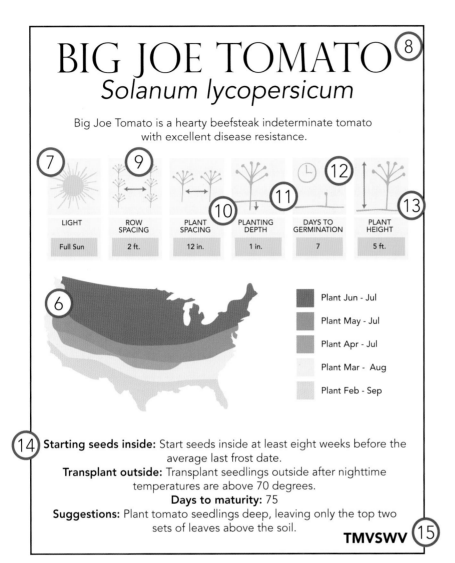

BIG JOE TOMATO ⑧
Solanum lycopersicum

Big Joe Tomato is a hearty beefsteak indeterminate tomato with excellent disease resistance.

⑦ LIGHT	⑨ ROW SPACING	⑩ PLANT SPACING	⑪ PLANTING DEPTH	⑫ DAYS TO GERMINATION	⑬ PLANT HEIGHT
Full Sun	2 ft.	12 in.	1 in.	7	5 ft.

⑥

- Plant Jun - Jul
- Plant May - Jul
- Plant Apr - Jul
- Plant Mar - Aug
- Plant Feb - Sep

⑭ **Starting seeds inside:** Start seeds inside at least eight weeks before the average last frost date.
Transplant outside: Transplant seedlings outside after nighttime temperatures are above 70 degrees.
Days to maturity: 75
Suggestions: Plant tomato seedlings deep, leaving only the top two sets of leaves above the soil.

TMVSWV ⑮

7 Light requirements

Most vegetables require full sun, but the tag will note the requirements.

8 The top of the seed packet

Usually has information about the type of plant you're growing. Indeterminate tomatoes keep growing and growing—like a vine—while determinate tomatoes stop.

9 Row spacing

Space needed between rows (if you're planting in rows).

10 Plant spacing

The amount of space required between individual plants.

11 Planting depth

The depth at which you'll plant the seed if you're sowing the seeds outside, as opposed to planting transplants.

12 Days to germination

The number of days between when you plant the seed and when it sprouts. Most vegetables require certain soil temperatures for germination. Radishes germinate in 50-degree soil, while tomatoes require warmer soil. You can buy soil thermometers to take the temperature of the soil.

13 Plant height

The height of the mature plant.

14 Starting seeds inside

Warm-weather vegetables are started inside to give them a head start on the growing season. All vegetables have a "days to maturity," which is the number of days between sprouting the seed and harvesting.

15 TMVSWV

These combinations of letters on seed packets indicate virus or disease resistance. In the case of this packet, the tomato is resistant to Tobacco Mosaic Virus and Spotted Wilt Virus.

How to Read a Hardiness Zone Map

When you shop for plants, you'll see information on the tags or in the plant descriptions that says "Hardy to zone 6" or "Hardy in zones 3–9." That information corresponds to the USDA hardiness zone map, which is based on the average annual minimum air temperature in an area. Some plants can survive in lower temperatures than others. The hardiness zone map provides a standard way for all plant growers to label their plants so that people shopping for plants can tell if a plant will survive the winter in their area.

If the information on the plant tag only says "Hardy to zone 6," you might want to find out other information about the other zones where the plant can grow. That's because the hardiness zone corresponds to cold, not heat. Take lilacs, for example. They are hardy to zone 3, but they don't like heat, and start suffering if they are planted in gardens in zones 7 or 8. They won't survive the heat in zones 9, 10, or 11.

Success Tip

If you want to grow perennials in container gardens, select perennials that will survive in a zone at least one number lower than yours. Perennials in containers aren't as protected from the cold as perennials planted in the ground.

Average Annual Minimum Temperature

■ Zone 1, below -50

■ Zone 2a, -45 to -50

■ Zone 2b, -40 to -45

■ Zone 3a, -35 to -40

■ Zone 3b, -30 to -35

■ Zone 4a, -25 to -30

■ Zone 4b, -20 to -25

■ Zone 5a, -15 to -20

■ Zone 5b, -10 to -15

■ Zone 6a, -5 to -10

■ Zone 6b, 0 to -5 ②

■ Zone 7a, 5 to 0

■ Zone 7b, 10 to 5

■ Zone 8a, 15 to 10

■ Zone 8b, 20 to 15

■ Zone 9a, 25 to 20

■ Zone 9b, 30 to 25

■ Zone 10a, 35 to 30

■ Zone 10b, 40 to 35

■ Zone 11, 40 and higher

Find Your Hardiness Zone

1   Look at the hardiness zone map and find your location.

See what color it is.

2   Look for that color in the color key on the right side of the zone map.

The color corresponds to your zone. Most plant tags do not get as specific as a or b (7a or 7b). They'll just say "zone 7."

3   Read the plant tag or description of the plant you want to buy to see if it will grow in your hardiness zone.

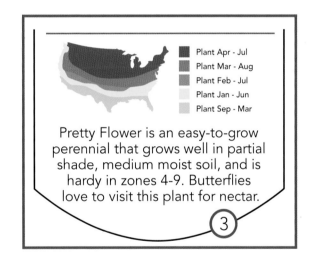

Plant Apr - Jul
Plant Mar - Aug
Plant Feb - Jul
Plant Jan - Jun
Plant Sep - Mar

Pretty Flower is an easy-to-grow perennial that grows well in partial shade, medium moist soil, and is hardy in zones 4-9. Butterflies love to visit this plant for nectar.

③

Know the Lingo

If the information says, "This plant will grow in zones 6 and lower," it means that the plant will grow in zones 6, 5, 4, and lower. The lower the zone number, the colder the winter. If you see information that says, "This plant will grow in zones 7 and higher," it means that a plant will grow in zones 7 to 11 (zones with numbers higher than 7). The higher the zone number, the warmer the winter.

How to Read a Fertilizer Label

Every fertilizer package has a label that tells the percentage of each of the main three nutrients (Nitrogen-N, Phosphorous-P, and Potassium-K) in the package. The label also shows what the fertilizer is made from, the amounts of other nutrients in the package, and how much of the package contents are other, non-nutrient ingredients. Here's how to read a fertilizer label.

Fertilizer Label

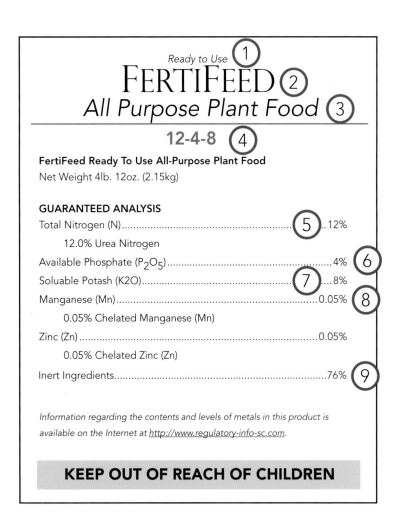

1   Type of fertilizer

"Ready to use" means that you can directly apply according to the instructions. Fertilizer marked as "concentrated" has to be mixed with water before spreading on plants.

2   The fertilizer brand name

There are different brands of fertilizer, just like there are different brands of clothes.

3   Intended use

This tells you which plants the fertilizer is for. Use different fertilizers for grass, vegetables, and flowers.

4 Fertilizer analysis

Every fertilizer has three numbers on the bag, separated by dashes. This is called the analysis, or sometimes the N-P-K number. The first number is the percentage of Nitrogen in the fertilizer, the second number is the percentage of Phosphorous, and the third number is the percentage of Potassium. This number is also a ratio. For example, a fertilizer with analysis 10-10-10 has a ratio of 1:1:1; in other words, the same percentage of available Nitrogen, Phosphorous, and Potassium in the fertilizer. A 12-4-8 fertilizer has three parts Nitrogen to one part Phosphorous and two parts Potassium.

5 Nitrogen content

This number indicates the percentage of Nitrogen in the contents of the package. In this example, a 4-pound bag with 12 percent Nitrogen has .48 pounds of Nitrogen.

6 Phosphorous content

This shows the amount of Phosphorous in the fertilizer.

7 Potassium content

This number shows the amount of Potassium in the fertilizer. This fertilizer example has .32 pounds of Potassium in a 4-pound bag.

If you need to apply 2 pounds of Potassium per 1,000 square feet, you would need 6.25 bags of this fertilizer.

8 Nutrients other than N-P-K

These are micronutrients, other nutrients that plants need in smaller amounts than Nitrogen, Phosphorous, and Potassium.

9 Other ingredients

Other ingredients make the fertilizer easier to spread.

Fertilizer FAQs

What's the difference between organic and synthetic fertilizer?
Synthetic fertilizer has the same primary nutrients (N, P, K) that organic fertilizer contains, but synthetic fertilizer has been made through chemical processes in a laboratory. Organic fertilizers are mixtures of naturally occurring ingredients, including items such as fish bone meal and worm castings (poop).

What is "weed and feed"?
Weed and feed products do double duty in the garden and lawn—they prevent weeds from sprouting and fertilize plants at the same time. These products don't kill weeds that have already started growing. The fertilizer in weed and feed products is usually slow-release fertilizer.

What is slow-release fertilizer?
Slow-release fertilizer is formulated so that the nutrients (food) are slowly released or made available to plants over a period of time—usually three to six months. You don't have to add extra fertilizer during this time.

What is foliar feeding?
You spray these products on the plant leaves, and the plants absorb the nutrients through their leaves.

How to Choose a Healthy Plant

Part of plant selection is preference—do you want to buy a plant while it's blooming or just about to bloom—and part of it is knowing how to find a healthy plant. If the plant's roots are happy, usually the rest of the plant is happy. However, you can't take the plant out of the pot to look at the roots while you're at the garden center. You can tell if a plant is healthy by looking at the top of it, if you know what you're looking for. Here's how to choose a healthy plant.

Look for Lush, Green Growth

You can tell which plant to select out of a group by looking at the whole group of plants. In the photo to the left, the plant on the right is losing its leaves and the tips of the vines are dying. You would leave that one at the store. The plant on the left is full of green leaves and new growth at the tips. It's the better choice.

Avoid Rotten Plants

Never buy a plant that looks rotten. It won't recover. Even worse, these plant pots, like those in the photo on the left, may have fungal diseases in them. If you bring the plant home, you'll bring home the diseases too.

Don't Worry About Deposits from Irrigation Systems

If the plants have a metallic sheen on their leaves (like you're looking at mirrored sunglasses), they have probably been watered with overhead sprinklers. The sheen is from something in the water. It will eventually wear off. If the plant is still growing and has firm flower buds, it is fine.

Just Grow With It!

Flowers: Open or Closed

When you buy perennials or chrysanthemums (perennials that are sometimes sold like seasonal annuals), buy plants that haven't bloomed yet. That way, you get to enjoy the flowers for longer. You'll get more enjoyment out of the mums on the right of the top picture that haven't opened yet. They'll give you a longer show than if you buy the plants on the left.

Browsing the Plant Sale Rack

At the end of the gardening season, you can get some good deals, particularly on perennials. The plants might look a little bit worse for the wear, but if they're cheap and they aren't obviously rotten and slimy, they're worth a try.

Trick Plants

The plant on the right looks dead, but it isn't. It is a sedge that is always brown, even when it is healthy.

Signs that a plant is healthy

- It's growing. Look for new leaves at the end of stems and branches. Sometimes new growth is a lighter green, and sometimes (in the case of roses) new leaves will be reddish.

- It looks "in proportion" with its pot. A healthy plant won't have roots growing out of the bottom of the pot, and it won't be spilling out of the pot.

- Unless the plant's leaves are supposed to be a different color (check the picture on the plant tag), mature leaves should be a nice, medium green.

Signs that a plant is not healthy

- The plant has lost its leaves, even though it isn't fall.

- The plant stems are mushy and rotten.

- The tips of the branches are dying. If a plant has a root problem, you can tell by looking at the ends of the branches. If the leaves are turning brown and dying, leave the plant at the garden center.

- The plant leaves are crispy, the edges are brown and dry, or the plant is droopy, all of which mean the plant hasn't had enough water.

Part Two: Gardening Basics

Gardening is less complicated than you might think, and knowing the correct techniques for a few basic, but important, aspects of plant care will take you a long way on the road to success. From knowing how to start seeds or plant seeds outside, to ensuring that your garden soil is healthy, these garden basics are essential building blocks for future success. The most important technique demonstrated in this section is how to water plants, which is probably the number one gardening technique you need to know how to do in order to grow happy, healthy plants. Learning how to water correctly, and a few other techniques, will make gardening easier and more fun. And gardening's supposed to be fun!

Know the Lingo

Look up the definitions of these terms in the glossary before reading through this part, and you'll have a leg up on your learning!

- Acidic soil
- Alkaline soil
- Brown materials
- Garden fork
- Garden lime
- Green materials
- Hose breaker
- Irrigation
- Nozzle
- pH
- Seed starting mix
- Soaker hose
- Soil knife
- Soil test
- Watering wand

How to Start Seeds

There is nothing more miraculous than planting a handful of seeds in bare earth, coming back a week or two later and seeing new green sprouts. How something as large as a sunflower can grow six feet tall in one season while starting from something as small as a sunflower seed is mysterious. Inside a seemingly dead seed, though, is a tiny dormant plant that's waiting for the right conditions to sprout. Even gardeners living in colder areas can start some plants from seed outside, and everyone can start seeds inside to get a jump on the growing season.

What You'll Need

- ☐ Seeds
- ☐ Seed starting mix
- ☐ Trowel
- ☐ Watering can
- ☐ Plant labels
- ☐ Pencil
- ☐ Seed starting tray
- ☐ Spray bottle with water

Instant Green Thumb

The first leaf or leaves that you see after a plant sprouts are called the "seed leaves." These are leaves that were actually curled up inside the plant seed, and grew and expanded as the seed sprouted. When you transplant your seedlings, you should wait until the plant has grown two more sets of leaves above the seed leaves.

Starting Seeds in Peat Pots

1 Peat pots are actually dried, compressed stacks of peat in small, biodegradable nets. The advantage to peat pots is that you don't ever have to remove the seedling transplants from the peat pots in order to plant. You can plant the seedlings—peat pots and all—directly outside. This disturbs the plant roots less, so the plant can get growing faster.

2 Drop the peat pots in water and let them soak for ten to fifteen minutes. They will expand to about the size of a small Dixie cup.

3 Put the peat pots in a plastic container without drainage. A Tupperware container works well. Prepare the peat pots for planting by using a sharpened pencil or bamboo shish kabob skewer to make a hole in the peat pot.

4 Plant two seeds per peat pot. Put the seeds in the holes you made with your pencil and pinch the top of the pot closed. To keep the peat pots moist, put some tap water in the bottom of the container they're sitting in once a week. Don't let the peat pots dry out. It's hard to re-wet peat once it gets dry.

Starting Seeds in Seed Trays

1 You can buy seed starting tray kits at garden centers or home-improvement stores. Usually you have to buy special seed starting mix separately. This is a lightweight soilless mix made especially for starting seeds. Never use regular garden soil, as this soil can have fungi in it that kills emerging seedlings. Use a pencil to poke holes for the seeds in each section of the tray in which you'll plant the seeds.

2 Plant one or two seeds per section of the seed starting tray. Then water the soil until it is as moist as a wrung-out sponge. Depending upon the size of the sections in the seed starting tray, you might or might not have to transplant plants into larger containers to grow before planting outside.

3 Cover the seed starting tray with the plastic lid or with clear plastic cling wrap. This will keep the seeds moist. The top of the lid may become moist with condensation as the seeds begin to sprout. The condensation is a good thing, because it means you'll have to water the seeds less.

4 Check on the seeds as they're sprouting. If the top of the soil is dry, mist them with a spray bottle or very lightly water them. (Misting is better than watering because it is less likely to wash the delicate seedlings out of their spots in the trays.) Don't ever let seeds dry out while they're sprouting, or they'll die.

5 When seeds have two or more sets of "true leaves," you can transplant them into larger containers. Moving them up to four-inch pots gives them room to grow and get larger and stronger before planting outside.

Peas are the first seeds you can plant outside in the spring. Some people even plant peas when there's snow on the ground. Here's how peas grow: first they sprout, then they grow longer stems and more leaves. Next, they flower, and after the flowers are pollinated, they form pea pods for picking.

Peas sprouting

Peas growing

Peas flowering

Peas fruiting

Sowing Seeds Outside

Some plants, particularly root vegetables like radishes, beets, and carrots, prefer not to be moved, so you should plant their seeds directly into the garden.

1   Use a trowel to dig a row in the garden soil outside. Dig the row about one to two inches deep.

2   Sprinkle the seeds in the row according to spacing instructions on the seed package. Some seed packets will advise you to sow the seeds "thickly." That means to sprinkle a lot of seeds in one area because the seeds don't sprout consistently. You can always snip off seedlings at the soil line to make room if more seeds than you need sprout and grow too close together.

3   Sprinkle seed starting mix over the seeds. While you can cover seeds outdoors with regular garden soil, seeds sprout more easily when they're covered with the lightweight seed starting mix. After covering the seeds, water them. Do not let the soil dry out until you see the seeds starting to sprout. If the seeds dry out while they're sprouting, they'll die.

4   Label the rows where you've planted seeds. Seed leaves can look similar to one another when they're sprouting, and you don't want to forget what you planted, where.

How to Improve Garden Soil

Almost no garden has perfect soil, so gardeners have to add materials called soil amendments to landscape beds. You can buy soil amendments or create them yourself. Garden soil is constantly changing. More soil is created daily by the millions of bacteria, fungi, insects, worms, and other creatures that live in the soil. These creatures eat leaves and grass clippings, flower petals, and twigs, breaking them down into soil particles and enriching the soil. Here's how to take care of your soil so that you have healthy plants.

What You'll Need

- [ ] Pitchfork
- [ ] Garden fork
- [ ] Soil test kit
- [ ] White piece of paper
- [ ] Soil amendments
- [ ] Yard debris
- [ ] Water

Instant Green Thumb

Composting is not mysterious! If you make a pile of leaves, grass, twigs, straw, newspapers, and kitchen leftovers, and let it sit long enough, it will turn into compost. Compost equals decomposition, a naturally occurring process. You can help speed the process, though. Read on to learn how.

How to Compost

1 Build a compost pile by layering green materials and brown materials like you'd make a lasagna. Start with chopped up dried leaves (you can run over them with the lawn mower). Then add grass clippings or kitchen scraps, and keep layering. The smaller the pieces you add to the pile, the faster they'll decompose.

2 Continuously add material to the compost pile—shredded newspapers, the stems of broccoli, last summer's dead annual flowers that you pulled up, even the Halloween pumpkin. Keep the pile "cooking" (a healthy pile will heat up) by using a pitchfork or garden fork to turn the pile and mix it up.

Grass clippings   *Kitchen scraps*   *Shredded newspaper*   *Leaves*   *Wheat straw*

Compost ingredients

There are two types of materials to add to compost piles. Green materials, which are high in Nitrogen, and brown materials, which are high in carbon. While there isn't a precise ratio of green to brown materials required in compost piles, if you add equal amounts of each over time, you'll get usable compost faster.

Brown materials

- Shredded newspapers
- Dried leaves
- Sawdust
- Wood chips
- Coffee grounds
- Paper bags
- Paper towels
- Twigs
- Tea bags
- Wheat straw

Green materials

- Grass clippings
- Weeds
- Green leaves
- Kitchen scraps
- Eggshells

Just Grow With It!

Don't throw meat on the compost heap! You can compost almost any natural material, but if you're composting at home, don't put any animal products other than eggshells in the compost pile. No meat, cheese, dairy, or lasagna leftovers.

Compost Troubleshooting: Smelly Piles

Smelly compost piles are usually too wet. You can fix this by adding more brown materials and turning the pile so that it can dry out. Throw some chopped leaves, straw, or shredded paper on the pile.

Compost Troubleshooting: Piles That Aren't Shrinking

As the items in the pile decompose, the pile will shrink. If the pile isn't shrinking, it isn't cooking. First turn the pile, then water it.

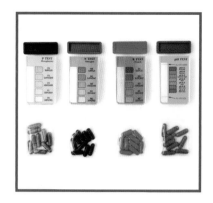

How to Test the Soil

Get a Soil Test Kit

You can get soil test boxes and forms from your local Cooperative Extension office. You can also purchase soil test kits at garden centers and home-improvement stores so that you can test the soil at home. These kits will allow you to test for the presence of Nitrogen-N, Phosphorous-P, and Potassium-K in the soil. Test the soil to see if anything is lacking *before* adding fertilizer, lime, or amendments other than compost to the garden.

1 Add soil to the kit from the area of the garden that you want to test. Then add water according to the instructions.

2 Add the indicator powder to the water in the container and shake the container to mix the soil, water, and indicator powder. (Usually the indicator powder comes in a capsule.)

3 Hold the container against a piece of white paper so that you can check the color of the water with the soil in it against the color key on the container. The color of the water will match one of the colors in the key on the container. The reading will tell you what is happening in the soil—acidic (low pH) or basic (high pH) soil, low Nitrogen levels, or high Phosphorous levels. After testing, you'll know what to add (or not add) to the soil.

Success Tip

You can pick up soil test boxes from your local Cooperative Extension office. Every test result will give you recommendations for adding Nitrogen, Phosphorous, or Potassium. Collect a soil sample to submit by digging clumps of soil from different areas of the garden, mixing them up, and submitting them for testing.

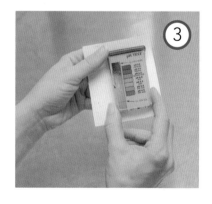

How to Fix Soil pH

The pH scale runs from 0 to 14. Most plants grow best in the range of 5.5 to 7.0, because nutrients in the soil are most available to plants at those soil pH levels. If your plants don't seem to be growing, check the pH and adjust it if necessary.

To Lower the pH

Soils with a pH lower than 5.5 are considered to be acidic. Soils with a pH above 7.0 are considered to be alkaline. To lower the pH of alkaline soils so that the pH is in the neutral range of 5.5 to 7.0, add aluminum sulfate according to package instructions. You can buy this at home-improvement stores and garden centers in the aisle with fertilizers and lawn care products.

To Raise the pH

Lawn grasses grow best when the soil pH is 6.0 or above. Homeowners in the eastern part of the United States, particularly, will need to use a rotary spreader to add lime to the soil periodically to raise the pH. Most vegetables don't grow well in acidic soils, so if the soil pH in the vegetable garden is below 5.5, add lime according to package instructions to raise the pH.

Just Grow With It!

If you don't have room for a compost pile, you can purchase bagged compost and soil amendments. (Amendments are beneficial materials to add to the soil.) Compost is beneficial for all soils. Compost improves drainage in heavy, wet clay soils, and helps sandy soils retain moisture. If your soil is high in clay (it's sticky when wet), consider adding a mixture of compost and sand. Earthworm castings (worm poop) are especially good additions for vegetable gardens.

How to Water Plants

There are plenty of conditions from which plants can recover—insufficient fertilizer, insufficient sun, improper pruning—but once plants go without water long enough to pass what is called "the permanent wilting point," they've reached the point of no return. Plants without enough water at the right time die quickly. Plants with too much water die slowly. (Their roots rot.) Lawns with too much water develop fungus problems. Watering really is a matter of life and death. Here's how to water the right way.

What You'll Need

- [ ] Garden hose
- [ ] Watering wand
- [ ] Sprinkler
- [ ] Ruler or measuring tape
- [ ] Straight-sided glass

Instant Green Thumb

The easiest way to tell if your plants need water is to look at them. Do they look saggy or droopy, sort of like they're slumped down in an office chair after too many hours of work? Are the stems limp and falling over? If so, the plants need water, and fast. As soon as you start seeing these signs of water stress, water the plants. Even a little bit will tide them over until you can give them more water later.

How to Water Landscape Plants

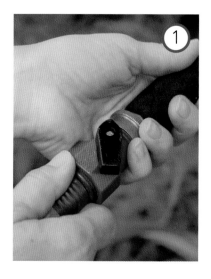

1 Prepare your watering tools by attaching the watering wand or hose nozzle to the hose and making sure that the water flow control is set to "off." It sounds basic, but if the water turns on and the nozzle is pointed at you, you'll be "inconvenienced," to say the least!

2 Turn on the water source. If you're using a spray nozzle, you won't need to turn the water on all the way. Remember to turn off the water when you're done! If you leave the faucet on, the pressure can build up inside the hose and the hose might burst.

3 Use the watering wand to water at the base of the plant. Direct the water into the soil next to the plant. If you spray the plant's leaves or fling water around, you waste water and increase the chances that fungal or bacterial diseases on one plant will spread, via water, to another plant. Watering wands with gentle water breakers are the best tools for hand watering because they slow the flow of water hitting the ground and keep the soil from splattering. Count to ten while watering each plant.

How to Water the Lawn

Lawn grasses need between one to two inches of water per week, depending on the grass variety and your soil type. You can consult a chart for grass type requirements, but it's better if you learn how to tell if your lawn is thirsty. If you observe these characteristics, your lawn needs water:

- Grass blades are folding over or curling up.
- The lawn has a grey tinge to it.
- The grass where you walk across the lawn stays lying down instead of bouncing right back up.

To make sure that you give your lawn enough water, but not too much, measure the amount of water your sprinklers spray during a specific amount of time.

1 Whether you're watering the lawn with an in-ground irrigation system on a timer or with a sprinkler that you move around, you can measure the output of the water system the same way. Set out a straight-sided container in the approximate middle of the area your sprinkler covers. (A short, straight-sided drinking glass works well for this.) Then let the sprinkler run for 15 minutes.

2 Use a ruler or measuring tape to measure the amount of water in the cup. You'll now know how much water the sprinkler puts out in 15 minutes. Set your irrigation timer (consult your owner's manual) or mark your calendar to water your lawn between one-half to one inch twice or three times a week, and you'll be on your way to a healthy lawn.

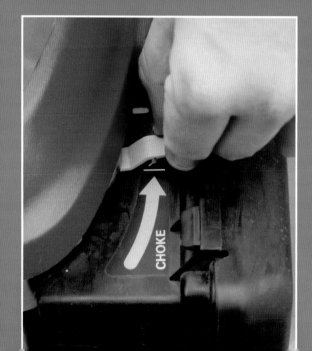

Part Three: Lawn Care

Consider your lawn a frame around the beautiful picture of your house and garden. If the frame is ratty or in poor shape, you'll notice the frame. If the frame is painted evenly and shows no signs of disrepair, you'll notice the picture.

Lawns are susceptible to a number of diseases and problems, particularly because the lawn is actually millions of the same type of plant growing close together, so problems spread fast! One thing that many people don't know about lawns is that you can prevent lawn problems (and save money on lawn products) by taking care of your lawn the right way. In this section, you'll learn the techniques to properly care for your lawn so that it will perfectly frame your garden picture.

Know the Lingo

Look up the definitions of these terms in the glossary before reading through this part, and you'll have a leg up on your learning!

- Acidic soil
- Blower
- Contact herbicide
- Drop spreader
- Fungicide
- Garden lime
- Grass clippings
- Irrigation
- Power edger
- Push mower
- Reel mower
- Rotary spreader
- String trimmer
- Turf
- Weed and feed

How to Mow the Lawn

Not everyone grew up mowing the lawn to make extra pocket money. If you find yourself renting or owning a house with a lawn that needs weekly attention, follow these instructions to mow the lawn properly. If you mow correctly, you'll prevent several common lawn problems, like weeds and diseases, from happening. Here's how to mow the lawn the right way.

What You'll Need

- [ ] Lawn mower
- [ ] Closed-toe shoes
- [ ] Broom or leaf blower

Instant Green Thumb

The roots of grass plants grow in proportion to the plant leaves (grass blades) aboveground. When you mow the grass at the tallest height recommended for its grass type, you allow the grass to develop healthy root systems that can better withstand drought. Taller grass also out-competes weeds by shading the soil and preventing weed seeds from sprouting. Here are recommended heights for common grass types:

- Bermudagrass: 1 to 2 inches
- St. Augustine: 2 inches
- Zoysia: 2 inches
- Bluegrass: 3 inches
- Fine Fescue: 3 inches

Step-by-Step

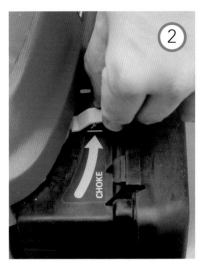

1 Set the mower height so that you're mowing at the tallest recommended height for your grass type. Most mower adjustment brackets are next to the front wheels, but consult your mower manual for specific instructions for setting your mower height.

2 Prime and choke the mower. The primer button is a small, soft plastic button on the top of the mower. Push it five or six times. Set the choke to the "cold" engine setting. If your mower doesn't have a choke, consult your manual for instructions.

3 While the mower is still on the sidewalk or driveway, hold down the safety lever at the top of the mower, set the throttle, and grab the starter cord. Pull the starter cord in a quick, jerking motion three or four times, until the mower starts. Once the mower is running, roll it over to the grass, slowly move the choke lever back to "warm," and begin mowing.

4 Start by mowing around the edge of the lawn first. This will give you somewhere to turn the mower at each corner. If you're using a bagging mower, move the mower back to the concrete or sidewalk and empty the bag. If you're using a mower with a side discharge, point the discharge toward the area you have not yet mowed, so that you can chop the grass clippings as you continue to mow.

5 Continue mowing the rest of the lawn. One trick to making sure that your lawn remains green and smooth is to change the direction you mow. One week, mow parallel to your driveway, the next week, mow perpendicular to the driveway. This prevents the mower's wheels from making deep ruts in the lawn.

6 While mowing each new row, place your mower so that it overlaps the previous row by 25 percent. By doing this, you make sure to cut the entire lawn evenly.

When you're finished mowing, always empty the mower bag and blow or sweep off the top of the mower with a leaf blower or broom. Use the broom or blower to sweep grass clippings that have blown onto the sidewalk or driveway back into the lawn.

Success Tip

When mowing the lawn, always wear closed-toe shoes, such as tennis shoes. Never mow in flip flops. If the mower, particularly a power mower, gets away from you, you need to have something between your feet and the mower blades!

How to Care for a Lawn Mower

The lawn mower is one of the most expensive pieces of maintenance equipment that most homeowners possess. It is also one of the most frequently used pieces of power equipment in the tool shed. To make sure that the mower is safe to use (remember—it has fast-spinning sharp blades!), care for it the right way. Here's how to take care of the lawn mower.

What You'll Need

- ☐ Broom or leaf blower
- ☐ Gasoline
- ☐ Mower engine oil
- ☐ Owner's manual

Instant Green Thumb

Stay safe while working with your lawn mower. Always follow these tips:

- Before doing any work on the underside of the lawn mower (dusting it off, inspecting it), disconnect the spark plugs. If you don't disconnect the spark plugs, the engine could start, and the blades could start spinning while your hands are touching them.

- Never tip your mower on its side to inspect the undercarriage when the mower has gasoline in it.

Mower Care Techniques

Filling The Mower with Gasoline

Always fill the gas tank of the mower while the mower is still sitting on the sidewalk or driveway (never in a closed room). That way, if you spill gasoline, you won't kill the grass and damage the soil. Fill the gas tank only 75 percent full so that there's room for the gas to expand.

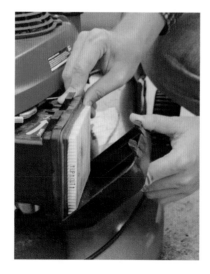

Checking the Air Filter

You should replace the air filter at the beginning of every season. It is a good idea to check the air filter once a month or so to make sure it looks clean and doesn't need to be replaced midseason. You can remove the air filter and tap it on the ground to dislodge some of the dust to extend its life.

Checking the Oil

Most lawn mowers have a dipstick as part of the oil cap. Remove the dipstick and look at the oil on the end, which should be clear to light brown. If it is any darker, you'll need to change the oil. Consult your owner's manual about how to change the oil, and recycle the old oil by taking it to a local mower or engine repair shop.

Refill the oil by using the right weight and type of oil for your mower. Your owner's manual will have information about whether to add two stroke or four stroke oil.

Cleaning Out the Bag and Undercarriage

Always empty the mower bag after you're finished mowing. (If you have a mulching mower, there's no bag to worry about.) Grass clippings make great mulch for your vegetable garden or are perfect additions to the compost pile. In the fall, use your mower and bag to chop up and vacuum leaves from the lawn.

Use a broom or leaf blower to clean off the top of the mower. Never hose off the mower, or you'll cause it to rust.

End-of-Year Maintenance

You can stop mowing when the grass stops growing for the year, which will be sometime between September and December for most gardeners. Run the mower until the gas tank is empty. Move the mower to a hard surface in a well-ventilated area, and drain the oil. Disconnect the spark plugs, and use a hard-bristle brush, an old rag, and a bucket of soapy water to clean off the underside and top of the mower. Add a fresh quart of oil to the oil tank and engine stabilizer to the gas tank. Never run water through the gas or oil tank to clean it.

How to Fix Lawn Problems

Your lawn and garden have as much to do with the value of your home as your home itself. You can have a green, healthy lawn without back-breaking work and using excess chemicals. Just use good lawn care techniques. When you have a lawn problem, always identify the problem before deciding upon the best solution. Here's how to properly maintain your lawn and fix common lawn problems.

What You'll Need

- [ ] Lawn mower
- [ ] Sprinkler
- [ ] Rotary spreader
- [ ] Garden hose
- [ ] Core aerator
- [ ] Weed killer (pre- and post-emergent)
- [ ] Gloves
- [ ] pH test kit
- [ ] Hard rake
- [ ] Soil
- [ ] Grass seed

Instant Green Thumb

Before trying to fix the lawn, examine your mowing habits (is the mower blade set high enough), watering habits (do you water deeply a couple of times a week (good) or for a few minutes every day (bad), and fertilizing habits (too much is not good). Give your lawn excellent care and many problems will go away on their own.

Problems and Solutions

Dog Spots

To fix dog spots, first flush the soil by watering the area twice a day for three or four days. Then, dig out the top two inches of soil and replace it with new garden soil. Next, sprinkle grass seed on top and water the grass seed twice daily until it sprouts.

Canada Geese

If you have geese in your yard more than a few days a year, you have a resident population, which is a problem. Geese eat a lot of grass, and will tear up your lawn. Then they leave lots of messy droppings. Dogs are great for chasing away geese. You can also spray the lawn with deer repellent or goose repellent.

Moles, Voles, and Grubs

These three problems are related. People mistake voles for moles and moles show up in lawns with grubs. If you have small holes all over your yard, voles are your problem. Voles eat plant roots, which can hurt plants. They also enjoy snacking on flower bulbs. The only way to get rid of voles is to get a cat. If you have tunnels on top of your lawn, you have moles, and the moles are there because there are lots of tasty Japanese beetle grubs in the lawn. Use milky spore powder (according to package instructions) to get rid of grubs, which will, in turn, help you get rid of moles.

Weeds

If your lawn is weedy, first adjust your lawn care techniques, because healthy grass will out-compete weeds. If you're mowing, watering, and fertilizing correctly, but still have weeds, you can use weed killers. Weed killers marked for "broadleaf weeds" will kill weeds such as dandelions without hurting the grass (as long as the temperature is below 75 degrees outside). You can use Roundup® in a spray bottle to individually spray big weeds too. To get ahead of the weeds, use pre-emergent herbicide or corn gluten to keep weeds from sprouting.

Moss

Moss is not necessarily a bad thing. In shady, damp areas, moss can serve as a stand-in for grass. It is, after all, green! Several different conditions cause moss to thrive, and whether you can get rid of the moss depends on whether you can control the conditions. Moss thrives in compacted, acidic soil (pH lower than 5.0) with low organic matter (generally, very clay-heavy or sandy soils). Damp conditions encourage moss, as do low air movement and shade. To eliminate moss, raise the soil pH by adding lime, prune the tree branches so that more light reaches the ground, and rake compost into the area.

Fairy Ring

Fairy ring is a fungus growing in the lawn. Most of the fungus is underground, but you can see symptoms of the disease in the lawn. Sometimes, you'll see a large green ring with brownish grass in the center. Other times, you'll see a perfect circle of mushrooms. It's hard to get rid of this problem, but you can help your grass survive it. The main problem is that the soil in the center of the circle becomes so full of fungi that it won't hold any water, and the grass dies. Fix this by renting a core aerator and aerating the center of the circle. Then rake compost into the aeration holes and water the lawn.

Brown Patch

Brown patch is another fungal disease. The damage can sometimes look like dog spot damage, but the patches are usually larger, and all of the grass in the affected areas isn't dead the way it would be in a dog spot. Brown patch is most often a problem in the summer when temperatures are above 70 degrees, and the grass stays moist for several hours at a time. (Lawns in the humid South suffer widely from brown patch.) Adjust the lawn watering schedule to water the lawn twice a week in the morning so that the grass has time to dry. Don't leave clippings on the lawn if brown patch is a problem.

Scalping

Scalping is a lawn problem caused by people that looks like a problem caused by bacteria or fungi. Scalping is when the mower blade is set so low that it doesn't just cut the top of the grass, it actually either rips the grass plant out of the lawn or cuts the plant so low that the plant stops growing. Scalping scars look like uneven strips of dead grass. The pattern could be irregular, depending on the mower pattern.

You can avoid scalping by setting the mower blade on a higher setting. Watch out for scalping problems with riding mowers. Once you sit on the mower, your weight will move the blade down slightly.

Heavy Foot Traffic

Some lawn grass types stand up to foot traffic better than others. For most homeowners, damage from people walking on the lawn isn't a major problem. If you have kids that like to play outside, you'll have more issues. If the grass near the swingset is dying, it's probably feet, not something else, killing it. You can stop trying to grow grass and mulch or build a path in the most heavily traveled areas. You can also plant grass that doesn't mind compaction from feet. In zones 7 and higher, plant bermudagrass or zoysia. In zones 6 or lower, plant perennial ryegrass or tall fescue.

Just Grow With It!

The right lawn care techniques go a long way toward preventing lawn problems from happening. Follow these tips for a healthy lawn.

- Use pre-emergent herbicide or corn gluten at the beginning of spring and fall to prevent lawn weeds from sprouting.

- Check herbicide labels carefully to make sure that you're using the right product. (Don't use a general herbicide that kills everything, or you'll kill both the lawn and weeds.)

- Set your lawn mower blade for the highest setting recommended for your lawn mower. This allows the grass to grow taller and shade weed seeds, which prevents the seeds from sprouting.

- Water the lawn deeply and infrequently. In other words, give the lawn 2 inches of water twice a week instead of one-half inch of water every day.

- Check the soil pH. If it is lower than 5.5, add lime according to the package instructions.

- Fertilize only according to recommendations for the type of grass you have. Extra fertilizer can cause grass to be weak and more susceptible to pests.

- Rent a core aerator and aerate the lawn once yearly in the fall to keep the soil from becoming compacted.

Aerated lawn

How to Fix Bald Spots in the Lawn

Bald spots in the lawn happen for a variety of reasons. You'll notice that areas where people frequently walk tend to wear down faster than other areas of the lawn. Sometimes a fungus will cause a section of lawn to die, or pets will relieve themselves and cause spots. The easiest and quickest way to fix bald patches in the lawn is with grass seed.

What You'll Need

- ☐ Soil
- ☐ Hard rake
- ☐ Grass seed
- ☐ Wheat straw
- ☐ Garden hose
- ☐ Sprinkler

Instant Green Thumb

If you live in zones 7 through 11, fix bald spots during the late spring and throughout the summer, when the most common lawn grass types are actively growing and will quickly fill in. If you live in zones 6, 5, 4, 3, or 2, patch bald spots in mid-spring or early fall, because lawn grasses there grow best during cool weather.

Step-by-Step

1 Start by using a hard rake to spread compost, topsoil, or garden soil in a one-half-inch layer covering the bald spot. While you can sow seeds directly in the bare spots, the grass will sprout more quickly and won't dry out as easily if it can start growing in loose, fresh soil.

2 Use a hand spreader to spread grass seed thickly and evenly over the entire area, slightly overlapping the edges of the grass that isn't covered with soil. When you're done seeding, the ground should look like it snowed lightly.

3 Sprinkle wheat straw, which you can get at garden centers and home-improvement stores, over the newly seeded area. This will help the seeds stay moist until they sprout. It's easy to grow new grass seed as long as you keep it moist. The biggest problem that people have when overseeding or replanting lawns is that they don't keep the grass seed moist while sprouting. The straw mulch helps eliminate that problem.

4 Grass seed must stay moist until it sprouts. Watering once a day for a couple of minutes isn't enough. Water the newly seeded area twice a day for ten minutes until the grass is at least an inch tall. Then water the newly seeded area three times a week for ten minutes. Don't mow the newly seeded area for at least two months. Newly growing grass is fragile, and foot traffic or mower blades could rip the new grass seedlings out of the ground.

Just Grow With It!

Overseeding is a lawn care technique that involves spreading new grass seed over the entire lawn, rather than just patching a bald spot.

In warmer climates (zones 6 and higher), the primary lawn grasses go dormant and turn brown during the winter. Overseed with annual ryegrass in September to enjoy a green lawn all winter. First, mow the lawn on the shortest setting. Then, use a rotary spreader to spread grass seed across the entire lawn. Water the grass seed daily until it sprouts. Then water the grass twice a week.

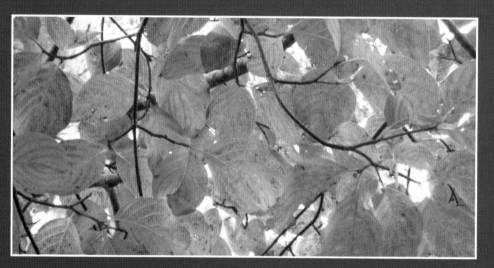

Part Four: Trees and Shrubs

What You'll Learn

How to Select a Tree

How to Plant a Tree

How to Prune a Tree

How to Select a Shrub

How to Prune a Shrub

How to Fix Tree and Shrub Problems

Trees and shrubs are the backbones of your garden and landscape. They anchor landscape beds, provide focal points, fill foundation planting beds next to your house, provide shade, and bloom to welcome the start of spring, summer, and fall. Evergreen trees and shrubs provide a bit of green in the landscape during the winter when everything else is dormant and bare. Trees have just as many interesting features as flowers, and they're an investment in your landscape that adds to your home's value. A yard filled with flowers but without any trees or shrubs will look bare. In this section, you will learn how to select, plant, and care for these important plants.

Know the Lingo

Look up the definitions of these terms in the glossary before reading through this part, and you'll have a leg up on your learning!

- B&B
- Bareroot
- Bud
- Deciduous plant
- Dormant
- Dripline
- Dwarf
- Evergreen
- Hand pruners
- Loppers
- New wood
- Pruning
- Pruning saw
- Shade
- Shrub
- Sucker
- Tree canopy
- Weeping

How to Select a Tree

Unlike annual or perennial flowers, trees aren't easy to move. Once you select and plant a tree, where it's planted is where it stays. In other words, it's important to choose trees carefully for your yard and garden. To pick out the right trees for your yard and garden, you should examine certain characteristics of the trees you're considering, including leaf color, flower color, and mature size. Here's what you need to know when you go shopping for trees.

What You'll Need

- ☐ Measuring tape
- ☐ Notebook and pen
- ☐ Notes about the area you want to plant the tree

Instant Green Thumb

Something to note when shopping for trees: the term "dwarf" on a plant tag doesn't mean that a tree will stay small. It means that the tree is a smaller, slower-growing version of the native species. "Dwarf" evergreens can still grow to heights of 20 or 30 feet over time, so make sure there's room for these trees to grow where you plant them.

Tree Characteristics to Consider

Redbud

Mimosa

Maintenance

If you don't enjoy yard work, you'll want to select trees that are easy to care for. Here are some choices.

Less (little pruning, few pest problems)
- Redbud
- Red maple
- Blackgum
- Hornbeam
- Katsura
- Alaska falsecypress
- Meserve holly
- Tree lilac
- 'Little Gem' magnolia

More (more pruning, messy, or disease-prone)
- Mimosa (messy)
- Southern magnolia (messy)
- Sweetgum (messy)
- Sycamore (messy)
- River birch (disease-prone)
- Hawthorn (disease-prone)

Crape myrtle

Redbud

Mature Size

The mature size of the tree is the size (height and width) the tree will be after it grows to maturity, sometimes in 20 to 40 years.

Small

Small trees grow no taller than 20 feet. These trees are good to plant in foundation beds (landscape beds next to the house), or to provide height in an island bed (larger landscape bed in the lawn).

- Serviceberry
- Japanese maple
- Star magnolia
- Kousa dogwood
- Crape myrtle

Medium

Medium-sized trees reach a mature height of 20 to 40 feet. They are great for landscape beds that extend away from the house at least 20 feet into the yard.

- Redbud
- Flowering plum
- Crabapple
- Carolina silverbell
- 'Little Gem' magnolia
- Golden raintree
- Zelkova
- Weeping cherry

Large

Large trees grow to heights of 50 feet or more, and make great shade trees. Give these trees lots of room to grow.

- Tulip poplar
- Beech
- Princess tree
- Sugar maple
- Sweetgum
- 'Autumn Purple' ash
- Red oak
- Honey locust

Princess tree

Carolina silverbell

Interesting Features

Trees have interesting features, including colorful berries, different leaf shapes, cool colors (even during the summer), and unique bark. Consider these attributes when tree shopping.

Flowers

Plant these flowering trees for extra pizzazz in your yard:

- Carolina silverbell
- Crape myrtle
- Star magnolia
- Flowering dogwood
- Cherry
- Smoketree

Magnolia

Fruits

Plant trees with interesting fruits only if you like to spend a lot of time in your yard or garden because fruits can be messy, meaning you'll have to spend some time cleaning them up, and you usually need to be close to the tree to observe and enjoy the fruits. Plant these for their pretty or unusual fruits:

- Magnolia
- Hornbeam
- Pawpaw
- Kousa dogwood
- Chinese fringe tree
- Golden raintree
- Osage orange
- Smooth sumac
- Burr oak
- Yellow birch

Dogwood

Leaves

Many deciduous trees (trees that lose their leaves in the fall) have interesting leaf shapes during the summer and pretty color in the fall, two good attributes for landscape trees.

- Blackgum
- Sweetgum
- Autumn purple ash
- Bald cypress
- Flowering dogwood
- Japanese maple
- Native American plum
- Sugar maple
- Aspen
- River birch

River birch

Bark

During the winter when there are no leaves on the trees, interesting bark is a gardener's best friend. These trees are beautiful, even in the winter.

- River birch
- Crape myrtle
- Paper birch
- Hornbeam
- Beech

- Paperbark maple
- Dawn redwood
- Scotch pine
- Sycamore
- Gumbo limbo

Evergreens

Evergreen trees (trees that keep their leaves all year) make excellent screening trees (for privacy or to block ugly views) and good backdrops for showing off other trees and flowers. When you go shopping for trees with evergreen leaves, you'll notice that not all evergreen leaves are "green." They are yellow, chartreuse, and even blue. Here are the best evergreen trees.

- Arborvitae
- Cryptomeria
- Douglas fir
- Western red cedar
- Atlas cedar

- White fir
- Colorado spruce
- Southern magnolia
- Falsecypress
- Camellia

Falsecypress

Carolina sapphire juniper

Atlas cedar

Serviceberry Tree

Serviceberry flowers   *Serviceberry fruit*

Just Grow With It!

Four-Season Trees

The absolute best trees for your yard are trees that have interesting characteristics all year long. Beautiful flowers, interesting fruits or berries, healthy green leaves in the summer, bright fall color, and bark that stands out in the winter all contribute to four-season function in the landscape.

The Tree That Beats Them All

If you have room for only one tree, or one more tree, plant a serviceberry. The species you should plant depends on where you live, but there's a serviceberry for almost every growing zone in the United States.

Why Are They So Great?

Flowers

Serviceberry trees bloom in late spring to early summer.

Leaves and Fruits

In the summer, serviceberry trees have lovely, kelly green leaves that show off their red or blue fruits.

Fall Color and Winter Twigs

Serviceberries have some of the most beautiful fall color of any tree. Their leaves turn bright shades of orange, red, and yellow. The leaves fall to reveal sculptural branches covered with smooth, gray bark.

Best Four-Season Trees

Not everyone wants a serviceberry tree in his yard. There are
some other excellent choices. Some are large, others are small.
Some bloom in the spring, others in the summer. All look
spectacular all year long.

- Crape myrtle
- Japanese maple
- Paperbark maple
- Bald cypress
- Southern magnolia
- Weeping beech
- Kousa dogwood
- Weeping cherry

How to Plant a Tree

While planting a tree isn't rocket science, there are myths and "old wive's tales" about the right way to plant a tree that can actually doom it before it starts growing. The size of the hole, the depth the tree is planted, and whether it is mulched all influence long-term tree health. Give your tree a leg up by following these steps.

What You'll Need

- ☐ Spade or shovel
- ☐ Wheelbarrow
- ☐ Watering can
- ☐ Mulch
- ☐ Tree

Instant Green Thumb

If it hasn't rained lately or your soil is particularly hard, water the area where you'll be planting the tree the night before digging the hole. It will be much easier to dig!

Step-by-Step

1 Use a shovel or marking paint to mark the area for the hole. The planting hole should be twice as wide as the tree's rootball.

2 Dig the planting hole. This hole should be just as deep as the rootball—no deeper! If you sharpen the spade before digging, this step will go faster.

3 Set the tree in the planting hole to check the depth. If the top of the rootball is lower than the soil line around the edge of the planting hole, add some soil back into the hole, pull the tree out of the pot, and replace the tree in the hole. You never want the crown of the tree (where the tree trunk meets the tree roots) to be below the soil line.

4 Fill in around the tree with the same soil that you removed from the planting hole. Do not add fertilizer or new topsoil. Water will move more easily and the tree will root properly if the soil in the planting hole and around the planting hole are the same.

5 Mulch around the tree, taking care to pull the mulch away from the tree trunk. Do not create a mulch "volcano" around the tree (by piling mulch up high around the trunk)—that just encourages insects and creatures that snack on tree bark to take up residence next to your delicious young tree.

6 Water the tree. Plan to water newly planted trees every three days (every other day if it is hot and dry). New trees don't need to be staked unless they're in areas prone to heavy rains and frequent winds. It can take a couple of years for newly planted trees to root all the way into the surrounding soil, so continue to monitor your tree for signs that it needs water.

Success Tip

Have you heard the saying "Plant 'em high"? Well, that refers to trees. Trees will settle a bit after planting. Always make sure that you finish the job with the top of the tree's rootball about three inches above the soil line. If you plant a tree too deep, the place where the tree trunk and the tree roots meet can rot, which will kill the tree.

How to Prune a Tree

Many trees grow just fine without regular pruning, but some trees will eventually require "limbing up" (removing the lower branches), will have branches that touch one another, or will have dead limbs that need to be removed. You can use a variety of tools, but if you're cutting branches that are larger than two inches in diameter, you should use a pruning saw and follow the "three-cut pruning technique." Here's how to do it.

What You'll Need

- ☐ Hand pruners
- ☐ Loppers
- ☐ Pruning saw
- ☐ Eye protection

Instant Green Thumb

Pruning trees is less confusing than it appears. If you're trying to decide what to remove from the tree, look at the tree, and remove branches in this order:

- ◆ First, remove any dead or diseased branches.

- ◆ Second, remove at least one of two branches that are rubbing against each other.

- ◆ Third, selectively remove branches to thin out the tree canopy, or top of the tree.

Step-by-Step

1 Make the first cut on the underside of the branch, about six inches from the tree trunk. You'll only cut one-fourth to one-third of the way through the branch.

2 Make the second cut farther out on the branch from the first cut. Cut the branch all the way off. The branch will probably break off while you're cutting it. That is why you made the first cut on the underside of the tree—to help the branch break in the direction you want without stripping the bark off the branch.

3 You can see the finished second cut, here. At the very bottom of the cut edge, you can see where part of the branch ripped. Heavy branches will rip further, often down to the cut on the underside of the tree. The cut on the underside of the limb keeps the branch from ripping all the way down the tree trunk and causing more damage. You never want to make a cut that strips the bark off of a tree branch, because all of the water and food in the tree travels up and down the tree right under the bark.

4 Cut off the branch stub remaining on the tree. Place the pruning saw just outside of the branch collar, which is the bark swelling between the branch and the main trunk. Saw all the way through to remove the stub. Do not cut the branch flush with the tree trunk, or you'll hurt the tree's chances of healing itself.

5 In this picture, you can see that there's still about one-fourth to one-half inch of branch left to allow the branch collar to heal. Never cover pruning cuts with tar, concrete, or sealant. The tree will heal itself if left alone. Sealant or tar creates a dark, moist environment that is perfect for bacteria to grow. Sealing a cut can actually hurt the tree, so resist the urge to "help" the tree heal. If you follow this pruning technique, the tree will heal itself.

Just Grow With It!

Have you ever heard the term "crape murder"? Gardeners in zones 7 to 10 can easily grow crape myrtles. However, many crape myrtles are victims of an unfortunate pruning technique, where all of the leafy branches are cut back to nubs at the end of trunks reaching about four feet off the ground. This technique, called pollarding, is used to create beautiful alleés of street trees in European cities, but it belongs in Europe. Crape myrtles can be pruned anytime from midwinter to early summer. If you let them grow, only removing branches that are smaller than your pinky finger, crape myrtles will become lovely vase- or fountain-shaped trees.

How to Select a Shrub

Shrubs are workhorses in the garden. They're the most common foundation plants (plants next to the house). Shrubs also can be pruned into "living walls" or hedges for privacy. Birds and other wildlife rely on shrubs for food and shelter. When everything else in the garden has called it quits for the winter, evergreen shrubs provide a bit of green to liven up the brown, drab landscape, and everyone loves flowering shrubs like hydrangeas, azaleas, and viburnums. Here's how to choose the right shrubs for your garden.

What You'll Need

- ☐ Measuring tape
- ☐ Notepad and pencil
- ☐ Notes about the areas for which you need a shrub

Instant Green Thumb

Here's how to instantly add excitement to your yard and garden—plant shrubs with colorful berries. Here's what to plant:

- Winterberry holly
- Beautyberry
- Blueberry
- Highbush cranberry
- Huckleberry
- Cotoneaster
- Firethorn
- Christmas berry
- Coffeeberry

Specimen Shrubs

Beautyberry
Bottlebrush buckeye

A specimen plant is a plant that "sticks out" (in a good way) in the landscape. A specimen plant might have beautiful flowers, vibrant berries, or a striking growth form. Usually, you plant only one or two specimen trees in the yard. Shrubs are typically planted in groups of three or more, though, so it isn't overkill to plant more than one spectacular shrub together. Here are some of the most interesting specimen shrubs. Plant these, and you're guaranteed a "What's that?!?" reaction from your neighbors.

- Beautyberry (berries)
- Bottlebrush buckeye (flowers)
- Hydrangea (flowers)
- Shrub roses (flowers)
- Weigela (flowers, leaves)

Shrubs to Plant for Privacy

Two types of shrubs offer privacy. Evergreen shrubs block ugly views in winter and summer. Thorny shrubs keep people from cutting through your yard. Here are the best of both.

- Barberry (thorny)
- Arborvitae (evergreen)
- Pieris (evergreen)
- Podocarpus (evergreen)
- Privet (evergreen)
- Rhododendron (evergreen)
- Azalea (evergreen)
- Firethorn (evergreen, thorny)
- 'Blue Boy' holly (evergreen, thorny)
- Loropetalum (evergreen)

Loropetalum

Shrubs to Plant Near the House

Shrubs planted adjacent to a house are called foundation plantings, and they have several "jobs" to do. Evergreen shrubs are a plus because they hide the bottom of the house! Plants with fragrant flowers are nice to plant near the front door, so you smell them when you arrive and leave.

- Korean spice viburnum (fragrant flowers)
- Tea olive (fragrant flowers)
- Falsecypress (bright evergreen leaves)
- Blue rug juniper (groundcover)
- Cotoneaster (evergreen, groundcover)

Korean spice viburnum

Bluebeard   *Shrub rose*   *Hydrangea*   *Weigela*

How to Prune a Shrub

Using correct pruning techniques ensures that shrubs are green from top to bottom. If you've ever had a problem with a shrub dying from the ground up, it's because not enough light is reaching the bottom leaves of the plant. That's 100 percent correctable with the right pruning technique. Knowing when to prune also ensures that you won't cut off the flowers before the shrubs bloom.

What You'll Need

- ☐ Loppers
- ☐ Hand pruners
- ☐ Safety glasses

Instant Green Thumb

Do you have hydrangeas that won't bloom? How about azaleas that only bloom at the bottom? What about viburnums that have green leaves, but no flowers? Chances are, you're pruning the shrub at the wrong time. Prune spring-blooming shrubs such as azaleas and forsythias right after they finish blooming. Prune summer-blooming shrubs such as hydrangeas and bluebeard after they start growing in the spring. Never prune in the fall.

Pruning Techniques

Reducing Shrub Size

Not every shrub that is too big for its britches needs to be pruned into a square or a ball. Hedges have their place, but so do beautiful, natural-looking shrubs. Azaleas are an example of this. To prune azaleas, hydrangeas, and other shrubs that grow quite large, put away the hedge trimmers and get out the hand pruners (for branches close to you) and long-handled loppers (for branches that are farther back in the shrub). Then, just cut the branches back as far as you want, making sure to cut back to a leaf. Stagger the heights of cut branches to give the appearance of natural growth. It's that simple!

Trimming a Hedge

When trimming a hedge or an individual shrub, the key is to make sure that the bottom of the shrub sticks out just a little bit farther than the top of the shrub. This ensures that light reaches the very bottom of the plant. To trim a hedge, hold the hedge shears (manual or electric) at a slight angle with the handles closer to your body and the tips of the shears farther away. You want a slight "pyramid" edge to the hedge when you're done pruning.

Maintaining a Hedge

Maintain the nice, even lines of the hedge by looking for sprouts sticking up from the hedge. Some plants require a full trim every year, but others can just be cleaned up periodically. Use hand pruners to remove sprouts that have grown faster and stick out farther than the rest of the shrub branches. Always remember to cut back to a leaf!

Just Grow With It!

Roses are shrubs, too, so rose pruning techniques can be used to prune other shrubs. Always cut a rose stem back to a leaf. Plants grow from buds nestled between the stem and the leaf. If you cut a stem two or three inches out from a leaf, you'll have ugly, bare stem hanging out. Whenever you prune, you can't go wrong if you cut back to a leaf.

Hybrid tea roses are a bit more complicated to prune, but you can't go wrong with them if you cut old (more than three years) canes (branches) all the way to the ground, and always prune the branches back to a bud on the outward-facing side of the plant.

How to Fix Tree and Shrub Problems

Many tree and shrub problems are cosmetic—the tree or shrub might not look pretty, but it will live through whatever's bothering it. Other problems are lethal. For example, if you accidentally cut all the way through the tree or shrub bark when you're trimming around them, you will have "girdled the tree," cutting off the flow of food and water up and down the trunk. There's nothing you can do to save the tree at that point. There are entire books about tree and shrub problems. Here are some of the most common problems and how to fix them.

What You'll Need

- [ ] Nitrile gloves
- [ ] Soaker hose
- [ ] Eye protection
- [ ] Dust mask
- [ ] Long-sleeved shirt
- [ ] Long pants
- [ ] Closed toe shoes
- [ ] Hand pruners
- [ ] Shrub rake
- [ ] Disease treatment products

Instant Green Thumb

There's one sure way to know the exact problem afflicting your trees and shrubs: take a piece of the affected leaf or branch to the professionals and have them diagnose the problem and give you treatment recommendations. Look up the address of your local County Extension office. You should be able to send them a sample (branches, leaves, or flowers) to get help and information.

Problems and Solutions

Blackspot

This fungus affects rose shrubs. You'll notice the fungus starting as black spots in the leaves. Eventually the leaves turn yellow and fall off. The best cure for blackspot is prevention. Prune roses so that there is space between shrub branches so air can circulate through the shrub. Deadhead roses and rake leaves and other debris from under the shrubs and throw it away. Prune off branches infected with blackspot and throw those away. (Never compost diseased plant parts.) Use soaker hoses or water roses at the base of the plants, because the disease spreads through water. You can also use sulfur products and specially formulated fungicides for roses to control blackspot.

Deer

Deer enjoy eating tree leaves and twigs as much as they like to munch hosta leaves and flower petals. You can tell if deer have been visiting if the branches and leaves have been chewed off trees from the ground to four or five inches above the ground. You can protect plants from deer by spraying them with deer repellent. Be sure to change repellent brands every six months. You can also wrap shrubs in deer netting during the winter.

Bagworms

Bagworms affect pine, spruce, juniper, cedar, and arborvitae trees. The adult moths lay eggs that survive the winter in cocoons that look like pinecones hanging on the trees. Eggs hatch in the spring and caterpillars eat the tree leaves. To prevent massive damage from the caterpillars, pick off the bagworm bags and burn them. You can also use insecticides to spray the tree when caterpillars are small. Read the pesticide label to be sure it's a product that kills bagworms.

Cedar Apple Rust

This pest needs apples and cedars to complete its life cycle. In the winter, the fungus lives on the cedar trees in galls (round swellings that look like orange, hairy ping pong balls). Spores from the cedar trees move to apple trees during the spring and cause yellow spots with black centers. As the fungus grows, what look like small hairs will grow on the leaves. To get rid of this pest, you have to eliminate either the cedars or the apple trees, or plant resistant plants. You can also spray with fungicides, but those are not always effective.

Iron Chlorosis

If you see trees and shrubs with shockingly bright yellow-green leaves and deep green veins (instead of evenly green leaves), the tree is probably experiencing iron chlorosis. Trees can live for a long time this way, but they'll be ugly and more susceptible to other pest problems. There are two ways to treat the problem: lower the pH of the soil by adding 5 pounds of sulfur for every 100 square feet of area around the tree, or spray the tree with what is called a "foliar spray" with iron in it.

Part Five: Flowers

What You'll Learn

Bright and colorful flowers are the candy of the garden. You can't help but smile when you look at an overflowing pot of petunias or catch a butterfly landing on a purple coneflower. But how do you decide, out of the thousands of choices, which flowering plants are right for your garden? It all depends on whether you want plants that bloom only for a few weeks, but come back year after year, or plants that bloom for months at a time but have to be replanted each season. Your choice also depends on whether you have sun in your yard or mostly shade. In this section, you'll learn how to select the right plants for your garden and how to care for them so they'll bloom beautifully.

Know the Lingo

Look up the definitions of these terms in the glossary before reading through this part, and you'll have a leg up on your learning!

- Afternoon sun
- Annual
- Biennial
- Bolting
- Bulb
- Cool-season annual
- Deadhead
- Diatomaceous earth
- Divide
- Dormant
- Full sun
- Host plant
- Liquid fertilizer
- Morning sun
- Naturalized
- Nectar plant
- Part shade
- Perennial

How to Select Annuals

No garden is complete without bright and colorful annual plants. Although annuals live for just one season, while they're in your garden, they'll bloom their heads off (or keep growing gorgeous, colorful leaves). Some annuals grow best in cool weather, while other annuals grow best in warm weather. You can change your mailbox, container, and landscape plantings with the season so that something is in bloom virtually at all times. Even if most of your garden is planted with perennials, always leave room for annuals.

What You'll Need

- [ ] Measuring tape
- [ ] Notepad and pen
- [ ] Trowel
- [ ] Mulch
- [ ] Watering can or hose
- [ ] Plants

Instant Green Thumb

Do you want your garden to burst with color like the flower displays you see at botanical gardens? Follow these tips:

- Pick out as many plants as you think you need, and then double that number.

- Plant annuals in odd numbered groups—preferably seven or more of the same plant per grouping.

- Buy flats, not six-packs. Big displays require lots of plants, but they provide big impact and enjoyment.

Tips for Planting Annuals

Buying and Spacing

Measure your planting area before you go shopping. Calculate the approximate square footage by multiplying length times width. Buy enough plants to cover one-third of the planting area at their current size (which will double or triple). When planting, leave two palms' width between each plant.

Planting

Planting goes faster if you remove all of the plants from their pots before you dig the holes. Only do this if you can plant on the same day you set out the plants. Always make sure that you dig down into the soil so the plant's rootball is in contact with the soil, not mulch, when you're finished planting.

Nasturtium

Osteospermum

Pansy

Plants for Cool Weather

Everyone can grow cool-weather annuals, but the timing is different depending upon where you live. If you garden in zones 7 or higher (8 through 11), you can generally plant cool-weather annuals in September or October, and they'll last through April. If you garden in zones 6 or lower (5, 4, 3, 2), you can plant cool-weather annuals in fall, but you'll have to replant in spring. Or, you can just wait to plant until March, and enjoy the cool-weather plants until June.

- Pansy
- Viola
- Osteospermum
- Alyssum
- Annual lobelia

- California poppy
- Snapdragon
- Calendula
- Nasturtium
- Ornamental cabbage

- Dusty miller
- Swiss chard
- Sweet William
- Sweet pea
- Forget-me-not

Success Tip

Enjoy cool-weather annuals by planting beautiful container gardens. Choose no more than two or three colors of flowers per container, and pack the container full of plants.

Calendula   Larkspur

Dusty miller

Snapdragon

Alyssum

Warm-Weather Annuals for Sun

Celosia

Salvia

Flowering tobacco

Warm-Weather Plants for Sunny Spots

When selecting annual plants and flowers to plant beside one another, look for details in one plant that are matched in other plants. That makes them good plants to put together.

There's an almost infinite variety of summer sun annuals. Plant these when nighttime temperatures are at least 60 degrees.

- Zinnia
- Marigold
- Sunflower
- Celosia
- Melampodium

- Annual salvia
- Petunia
- 'Diamond Frost' euphorbia
- Ageratum
- 'Prairie Sun' rudbeckia

- Cosmos
- Scaevola
- Angelonia
- Portulaca
- Verbena

Success Tip

Plant cool-colored flowers—purple, blue, green, and white—for a soothing, calming oasis in the garden.

Rudbeckia

Scaevola

'Diamond Frost'

Petunia

Warm-Weather Annuals for Shade

Persian shield · *Angel wing begonia* · *Torenia* · *Impatiens*

Warm-Weather Plants for Shady Spots

These plants thrive during hot summer days, but they need to be planted in the shade. Plant white flowers or plants with white leaves to brighten up dark, shady corners.

Some sun annuals can tolerate a bit of shade, but most shade annuals will bake if they're planted in the sun. Enjoy these flowers in your garden, but plant them where they get no more than morning sun (from 6 to 9 am).

- Angel wing begonia
- Rex begonia hybrids
- Caladium
- Coleus

- Geranium
- Impatiens
- Madagascar periwinkle
- Persian shield

- Torenia
- Polka dot plant
- Perilla
- Fuchsia

Success Tip

Plant Persian shield, coleus, polka dot plant, and rex begonia hybrids for their pretty leaves.

Coleus · *Madagascar periwinkle* · *Polka dot plant* · *Rex begonia hybrid*

How to Care for Annuals

Annual plants live for one growing season. These plants make up for their short lives by blooming continuously for four, five, or even six months. Make sure that you get the most out of your colorful annual plants by giving them the best care. Using these simple techniques in the garden will help you keep your plants blooming and growing for months.

What You'll Need

- [ ] Fertilizer
- [ ] Hand pruners, scissors, or snips
- [ ] Shrub rake
- [ ] Garden hose
- [ ] Watering wand
- [ ] Bucket
- [ ] Garden twine
- [ ] Plant stakes

Instant Green Thumb

When the petals fall off and the flowers fade, the plants start producing seeds, which is the plant's signal that life is over. You need to trick the plant into continuing to bloom by cutting off the old flower and preventing seed formation.

Get out the scissors or pruners and shout, "Off with their heads!"

Annual Care Techniques

Deadhead Annual Flowers Weekly

Use your scissors, snips, or hand pruners to snip off dead flowers. Always cut and remove the flower stem at the place where it meets the main plant stem. If you only cut off the flower, you'll have ugly stems hanging around. New growth only sprouts from buds along the main stem.

Pinch Off Flowers as Needed

Coleus is a popular annual plant with brightly colored leaves. Pinch off coleus flower stalks when they sprout so that the plant stays neat and tidy. If coleus gets too large, just cut off the top half of the plant stems. They will resprout.

Fertilize

Liquid fertilizers (including organic fish emulsion) come in concentrated forms that you mix with water and apply to the soil around plants. Some concentrates are poured into watering cans and mixed, while others can be spread by using hose attachments that do the mixing for you. Slow-release fertilizers include blood meal and bone meal (organic), and pelletized fertilizers (non-organic). Spread these fertilizers on the soil around the plants, following package directions for amount and frequency (generally every two or three months). With fertilizer, more is not better! Always read the instructions so you give the plants the right amount.

Pull Up and Replant

Part of annual flower care is making the "seasonal switch." Starting in September (in zones 6 or higher) or April (in zones 5 and lower), you can plant pansies, flowering kale, snapdragons, and other cool-weather loving plants to enjoy during cooler weather. Once nighttime temperatures remain above 60 degrees, you can plant warm-weather flower transplants, including marigolds, annual salvia, petunias, and more. Pull out the old flowers or use pruners to cut them off at the ground.

Water

The difference between garden beds with big, beautiful annual flowers and pathetic, spindly, half-dead flowers is often water. You need to water more frequently right after you plant annual flowers, as much as daily for the first two or three weeks, and every three or four days for the first six weeks. That's because it takes a while for the plants to grow roots into the surrounding soil, where there's extra moisture. After six weeks, you can water plants once a week unless it is over 80 degrees every day without rain for a week or more. Count to ten while watering each plant, and aim the water at the soil right next to the plant rather than onto the leaves.

How to Select Perennials

Perennials come back year after year, so it's important to choose them carefully, or you'll spend a lot of time digging things up and moving them around. Just like annuals, perennials have specific light requirements, water requirements, and space requirements. When shopping for perennials, always read the plant tags and create groupings of plants that have the same needs. Here's how to choose perennial plants.

What You'll Need

- ☐ Notepad and pen
- ☐ Measuring tape
- ☐ Notes about planting area

Instant Green Thumb

Steer clear of deer! If you have deer problems in your area, plant these perennials, which deer find unappetizing.

- Yarrow
- False indigo
- Purple coneflower
- Joe Pye weed
- Bee balm
- Coral bells
- Perennial salvia
- Lamb's ear
- Yucca

Tips for Selecting Perennials

Understand Your Choices

At most garden centers and home-improvement stores, you'll find every variety of one kind of plant grouped together. You'll see ten different colors of coral bells, eight different sizes of hosta, and so forth. Don't let the choices overwhelm you! Start with one type of plant, choose the color you like the most, and go from there.

Take Plants for a Test Run

The best way to see if the plants you've selected look good together is to take them for a test run in the store. Arrange your plants in your shopping cart or find an empty spot at the store and set the plants out the way you'd place them in your garden.

Many of your favorite herbs are perennials. For a unique twist on the traditional sun perennial garden, plant an herb garden. These perennials like full sun and well-drained soil.

- Lavender
- Sage
- Oregano

- Thyme
- Rosemary
- Sorrel

- Marjoram
- Tarragon
- Bay

Check the hardiness zone for your area against the plant tags. Some herbs (such as rosemary) are perennial in zones 6 and higher, but need to be brought inside in zones 5 and lower during winter.

Just Grow With It!

Certain rascally plants need to be kept under control, but that doesn't mean you can't grow them. Mint is a prime example. If you plant it in your garden (in the ground), it will quickly take over. However, you can successfully grow mint in a pot, which will keep it from spreading through your entire garden. Place the pot in an area of partial sun near the house and water it weekly. Mint likes moist soil.

Mint   *Chives*   *Sorrel*   *Thyme*   *Sage*

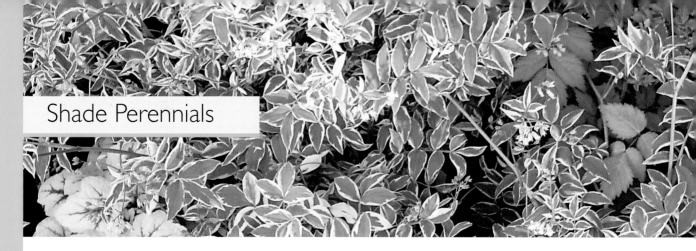

Shade Perennials

Shade gardens don't have to be masses of hosta (though hosta are easy to grow, which is why they're popular). Plant variegated (green-and-white) plants in the darkest corners of your shade garden to brighten it up. Use groundcovers under trees where grass won't grow.

Shade Perennials with Interesting Flowers

- Columbine
- Virginia bluebells
- Goatsbeard
- Toad lily
- Lenten rose
- Leopard plant
- Bleeding heart
- Bigroot geranium

Shade Perennials Grown Primarily for Leaves

- Hosta
- Siberian bugloss
- Coral bells
- Epimedium
- Lungwort
- Ferns
- Solomon's seal
- Wild ginger

Groundcover Shade Perennials

- Ajuga
- Pachysandra
- Lirope
- Creeping jenny
- Periwinkle
- Lily of the valley
- Sweet woodruff
- Hardy begonia

Success Tip

One way to "cheat" the system a bit when selecting plants and deciding where to plant them is to create what is called a "microclimate." Plant toad lilies, which like water, near your bird bath so they get extra moisture.

Virginia bluebells   Spiderwort   Japanese painted fern   Bleeding heart   Toad lily

Astilbe

Lungwort

Lenten rose

Groundcovers

Groundcovers are fast-growing perennials that can take the place of lawn, particularly in shady areas.

Don't limit your groundcover garden to short plants. Any fast-growing plant that takes the place of grass can be considered a groundcover.

Columbine

Gooseneck loosestrife

Creeping phlox

Solomon's seal

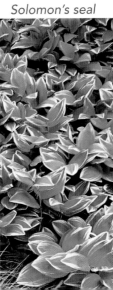

Sun Perennials

Perhaps the largest variety of plant choices abound in the sun perennial section. You can find plants in every color, height, and size for your sun garden. Here are some favorites in different categories.

Drought-Tolerant Sun Perennials

- Salvia
- Sedum
- Hens and chickens
- Thyme
- Mexican sage
- Russian sage
- 'New Gold' lantana
- Hardy ice plant

Tall Sun Perennials

- Yarrow
- Little bluestem
- Miscanthus
- Switchgrass
- Coneflower
- Swamp sunflower
- Swamp hibiscus
- Giant rudbeckia
- Eupatorium

Low-Maintenance Sun Perennials

- Black-eyed Susan
- Daylily
- Amsonia
- False indigo
- Blazing star
- Penstemon
- Gaura
- New England aster

Success Tip

While shopping look for plants with multiple stems. Daylily, yarrow, sedum, phlox, and bee balm plants can all be split in two as long as the plant has four or more stems. That gives you more for your money!

| Coneflower | Sedum | Anise hyssop | Bee balm | Daylily |

Pincushion flower

Yarrow

Hardy ice plant

Blazing star

Ornamental Grasses

Ornamental grasses are perennials that instantly transform a garden. Plant an ornamental grass to add movement and flow to the garden that wasn't there before. There are short and tall ornamental grasses, grasses that like sun, and grasses that love shade. You'll find one that fits your garden perfectly.

Aster

Sea thrift

Gaura

Sneezeweed

How to Care for Perennials

The no-maintenance garden is a complete myth, but if you want flowers and you want "easy," perennials are the way to go. You can do as much or as little with perennials as you want. Some people do all of their garden cleanup in the spring, while others meticulously deadhead every single day. Find a happy medium in between and your perennials will look great all year long.

What You'll Need

- ☐ Hand pruners
- ☐ Bucket or wheelbarrow
- ☐ Garden hose and watering wand
- ☐ Spade
- ☐ Garden forks

Instant Green Thumb

These plants require no deadheading and look good from the first spring growth through the first heavy snowfall. Look for them the next time you go shopping.

- Hosta
- Daylilies
- Ornamental grasses
- Sedum
- Russian sage
- Blazing star
- Hardy ice plant
- Artemisia
- Amsonia

Perennial Care Techniques

Garden Cleanup

To be safe instead of sorry, cut back perennials when they're fully dormant—in the winter or early spring. Simply chop them all the way to the ground and throw your clippings in the compost pile.

Pinching or Pruning

Get mums to bloom in the fall by pinching off the flower buds during the summer. Chrysanthemums, Joe Pye weed, bee balm, New England asters, phlox, heliopsis, balloon flower, and helenium can all be cut back by one-third in the spring to promote bushier growth and later flowering.

Watering

Most perennials don't need a lot of extra water after they've been in the ground for a year or two. However, if your area is getting less rain than is typical or the days are consistently over 85 degrees, you will have to water at least once a week during the growing season. The best way to water is by directing the water stream to the base of the plant. That puts the most water where the plant can get it—by the roots. If you need to set up a sprinkler, leave it on the same place for thirty minutes to an hour once a week to give plants a good soaking.

Deadheading

Deadheading is the process of removing faded flowers from a plant. Some perennials will reward you with additional flowers if you cut back their dead flowers. Others won't rebloom, but the plants look so much better after you cut off the old flowers. Where to cut back depends on the type of plant. Some plants sprout flowers along their stems. Once you cut off the top flower stem, new buds will sprout along the stem from between the stem and the leaf. (The blanketflower, pictured, does this.) Other plants do not resprout from the same stem as the flower. When those plants stop flowering, you can cut the flower stems all the way back to the leaves at the base of the plant.

Success Tip

Love lavender? Don't cut lavender back in the fall, and wait until new green growth emerges in the spring. Once the flowers bloom, you can clean up the plant by cutting the flower stems back to the plant leaves.

Dividing Perennials

Some perennials merely tolerate being divided, while others actually grow better after they've been divided. Still others respond poorly to or never require division. If you've noticed your perennials have started to bloom less or have a dead spot in the center of the plant clump, it is time to divide.

Plants to divide with the double fork or fork and spade technique include:

- Yarrow
- Aster
- Coreopsis
- Daylily
- Sneezeweed

- Coral bells
- Salvia
- Phlox
- Bee balm
- Penstemon

- Hosta
- Black-eyed Susan
- Chrysanthemum
- Artemesia
- Ornamental grasses

These plants can all be divided in the spring or the fall. Peonies and iris are divided in the fall, and spring-blooming bulbs are divided as soon as their foliage dies back after blooming.

Step-by-Step

1 Dig up the plant that you want to divide. Dig all the way around the plant clump, about four inches away from the edge of the plant. If you water the plants you're planning to dig up and divide the night before you're dividing them, they'll be easier to dig up.

2 Divide the plant with either a spade or two gardening forks. Garden forks work well for plants like daylilies because they have relatively small roots. Hostas have large roots, and ornamental grasses are often so dense that it is impossible to pry pieces of the plant apart with the forks, so you might have to use a spade to chop the plant apart.

When using a spade, put the spade in the center of the plant clump and chop the clump in half. Plants are tougher than you think, so don't worry about hurting them. Sharpen the spade before chopping—you'll be glad you did!

3 To divide with two forks, put the forks back to back in the center of the plant clump, push both down, and pry apart.

Replant the divided halves immediately, or put them in pots or plastic bags, and give them to friends. Plants that have been divided shouldn't be left out of the ground for more than a day. The tiny root hairs on their roots (which soak up most of the water a plant uses) have been disturbed, and the plants need to get back in the ground to grow new ones.

Peony

Iris

Just Grow With It!

Two plants have special needs when it comes to division. Here's how to divide peonies and iris.

Peonies

The secret to beautiful blooming peonies is not to bury them under a thick layer of mulch. If their fleshy roots aren't just under the soil, they won't bloom. After they bloom, cut off the flowers and let the leaves remain until they turn brown or yellow. Peonies go dormant in midsummer, at which point you can cut off the leaves. If you want to divide peonies, dig them up in the fall and slice the roots apart with a clean knife. Replant with the top of the root just one-half to 1 inch under the soil.

Iris

Bearded iris is another plant that doesn't like to be buried. Always make sure that the tops of the iris rhizomes (their fat, fleshy roots) are exposed to the sun. To divide iris, dig them up in August, and cut the rhizomes apart with a sharp knife. Replant with the rhizomes exposed, and remember to water!

How to Stake a Plant

Tall plants with big flowers on thin stems (peonies, lilies, sunflowers) generally need to grow around other plants for support, or they need to be staked so they don't fall over. The *easiest* way to stake a plant is to gather the whole plant, put a string around the middle, and cinch it. But that is not the best way to stake plants, unless you want your beautiful clump of lilies to look like they ate too much for lunch and are wearing a belt that's now too tight. Here's how to stake your plants.

What You'll Need

- [ ] Scissors
- [ ] Twine
- [ ] Plant stakes

Instant Green Thumb

To easily stake your cutting garden plants, which are generally tall plants with large flowers, create a framework for the plants to grow through at the same time that you plant them.

Use tall stakes and twine to create a web for the plants to grow up through. This technique is like weaving your own spider web around the stakes. It is similar to the staking technique on the opposite page, but for cutting gardens, you make the web before the plants have started growing.

Stakes vs. Cages

Stakes

Stakes are best for plants with one to seven tall main stems. Vegetables that grow single stems and bear heavy fruit, like peppers and eggplants, also benefit from being staked. Leave a little "breathing room" between the stake and the stem when you tie the stakes.

Cages

Cages come in a variety of shapes and sizes. Standard aluminum tomato cages can be used for other large vegetables. Peony cages are metal rings on legs, and may or may not have a gridlike support in the interior of the ring. Place cages when the plants are just sprouting.

Staking Tall, Floppy Plants

1 Place several stakes in and around the plant clump to serve as a framework and as individual supports. If one branch is particularly large and floppy, put one of the stakes next to it, about an inch away from the plant stem.

2 Start creating a web of string between the stakes. Try to pull the string as taut as possible between stakes, without bending the stakes. You can create as many crisscrossing strings as you'd like. The more string, the more support for the plants growing through the web.

3 You can tie individual stems to stakes with longer pieces of twine. This lets the stems "lean" as if they're naturally growing but still gives them individual support.

4 When you're finished creating your web of string and tying heavy individual stems to the stakes, your plants will be standing upright. As the plants grow, their foliage will hide the stakes and string. If the stakes are much taller than the projected size of the plant, you can cut them shorter with hand pruners.

Just Grow With It!

Bamboo or metal? Plastic or wood? Which plant stakes are the best plant stakes? You can buy natural bamboo stakes and stakes that have been painted green. Wood stakes are almost always made out of pine or a light-colored wood. Metal stakes are sometimes painted with a powder coat or covered in plastic. Light-colored stakes will "stand out" more in the garden. Of course, you can always paint them dark green or black. Metal and plastic stakes last longer than bamboo and wood stakes, but they all should last at least three years or so.

How to Plant a Perennial Sun Garden

Perennnial sun gardens aren't just beautiful, they're also easy to care for, a good investment (plants come back every year), and they lure birds and butterflies to your yard. Don't be afraid to design and plant your own garden—it's easy. Begin by selecting plants with a variety of heights, leaf textures, and flower colors. If they look good in your cart at the garden center, they'll look good planted together at home!

What You'll Need

- [ ] Tape measure
- [ ] Pencil and paper
- [ ] Hard rake
- [ ] Spade or shovel
- [ ] Garden trowel
- [ ] Compost or garden soil
- [ ] Mulch
- [ ] Plants
- [ ] Hose and watering wand

Instant Green Thumb

These sun-loving perennials thrive in almost every climate, are easy to grow, and are always available at garden centers. When planning your perennial sun garden, add these to your list:

- Bee balm
- Black-eyed Susan
- Coneflower
- Coreopsis
- Daylily
- Phlox
- Salvia

Step-by-Step

1 Measure the area where you're planning to plant the garden. Take length and width measurements and multiply them to get the square footage of the planting bed. You'll use these when calculating the amounts of soil, mulch, and plants to purchase for the garden bed.

2 Add two inches of soil or compost to the bed. To determine the total cubic feet needed, multiply the area of the bed (length x width) by two and divide by twelve. (For three inches of mulch, multiply the entire area of the bed by three and divide by twelve.)

3 Use a 4 tine claw or hard rake to mix the soil into the planting bed. In new housing developments, topsoil is scraped off and sold. Adding compost or garden soil replenishes nutrients and helps plants grow.

You might have heard the term "double digging" before. That's when you dig out all of the soil in a planting bed, mix it up with compost, and put it back. It is a lot of hard work, so it's a good thing that science has proven that it's unnecessary. Rototilling and double digging disrupt earthworms and other soil creatures, so add compost on top, rake it in, and leave it alone!

4 Set the plants out where you want to plant them. Stagger the plants so that they aren't arranged in straight lines. You can also create groupings with one of each type of plant and repeat the groupings in several places throughout the flower bed. If you know you'll have time to plant on the same day that you set out the plants, take all of the plants out of their containers before you set them in the planting bed—you'll save yourself a lot of time.

5 Dig the planting holes just as deep as the rootballs of the plants. If you're planting larger perennials (plants in gallon-sized containers), use a spade or shovel for quick work. Really pay attention to the depth of your planting hole. Perennials can't handle being planted too deep. The top of the rootball of a plant should be level with, or just slightly higher than, the ground around it.

6 Mulch the completed flower bed by spreading a layer of mulch two or three inches deep. Make sure that the mulch is slightly pushed away from the plant stems. Water the flower bed deeply by counting to ten while watering each plant, then repeat, again counting to ten on each plant. You'll need to water the plants daily for the first couple of weeks. After the first month, you can water the plants twice a week.

Success Tip

Read the plant tags when you shop for plants and choose plants that have the same water needs. Plant low-water plants with low-water plants, and plants that like staying moist with plants needing the same.

Just Grow With It!

Designing your own garden is easier than it seems. Decide upon a color scheme. Will it be all warm colors (red, yellow, orange, pink) or cool colors (purple, blue, lavender), or a combination of both? After deciding upon colors, look at leaf textures. Choose some plants with large leaves and others with small, fern-like leaves. Last, tackle form. Pick out some plants with stiff, upright growth habits (salvia, phlox) and others with softer, draping growth habits (ornamental grasses, daylilies). Mix and match, plant in odd numbers, and you'll grow a beautiful garden.

Bee balm

Purple coneflower

Just Grow With It!

Perennial sun gardens can do double duty as butterfly gardens, and what better way to enjoy your garden than by welcoming these "flying flowers"? To lure the most butterflies, you'll need to plant two types of plants: host plants and nectar plants. Nectar plants feed the adults (what we call butterflies). The adults then lay their eggs on nearby host plants, the eggs hatch into caterpillars, the caterpillars eat the host plants, and the cycle continues. If you're more interested in visiting butterflies than munching caterpillars, you can skip the host plants and go for nectar plants exclusively.

Host plants

- Dill
- Fennel
- Milkweed
- Parsley

Nectar plants

- Coneflower
- Phlox
- Black-eyed Susan
- Coreopsis

Coreopsis   *Salvia*   *Phlox*   *Daylily*

How to Plant a Perennial Shade Garden

New gardeners sometimes worry when most of their available gardening space is in the shade, but shady conditions are no cause for alarm. There are lots of interesting plants for shade gardens, and the greens, whites, and silvers of most shade plants serve as a soothing backdrop for the occasional pop of color from flowers. Here's how to plant a shade garden.

What You'll Need

- ☐ Plants
- ☐ Garden soil
- ☐ Mulch
- ☐ Trowel
- ☐ Hard rake
- ☐ Garden hose
- ☐ Watering wand or nozzle

Instant Green Thumb

Plant these no-fail shade garden plants:

- Hosta
- Leopard plant
- Coral bells
- Columbine
- Lenten rose
- Goatsbeard
- Bearded iris
- Lirope
- Ferns
- Solomon's seal

Step-by-Step

1 Measure the area where you want to plant. (Remember—length times width equals area.) You can also measure from the tip of your middle finger to your elbow, so that you have a "yardstick" with you at all times. At the garden center, you'll want to get plants that cover about one-third of your bed area.

2 Spread two inches of compost across your planting area. You can buy bagged manure, mushroom compost, and other soil amendments. Use a 4 tine claw or hard rake to mix the compost into the top layer of the soil.

Just Grow With It!

Shade gardens are all about texture and light. Shady corners are dark, so to make your plants pop, you'll need to add contrasting textures and colors. Look for plants with variegated (green-and-white) leaves, because the white color will help brighten the shady area. For added light, tuck a few white impatiens or white caladiums in between your shade perennials.

Plants with contrasting textures add a bit of excitement too. Plant hostas, which have large, solid leaves, next to Japanese painted ferns, which have lacy, cut-out leaves, to create a garden vignette worth admiring.

3 Place your plants where you want to plant them. Pay attention to spacing requirements on the plant tags (perennials will double or triple in size eventually), and move the plants around until you have the look you want. In a shade garden, it's fun to mix colors and textures, so enjoy this "on the ground" design phase.

4 Remove the plants from their containers and plant them. If the plant looks especially rootbound (the roots are a hard, matted cluster in the pot), you can break them up with a trowel or pruners. The planting hole should be just as deep as the plant's rootball but no deeper.

Success Tip

How do you know which plants like shade when you're shopping at the garden center? Start by looking for plants under awnings or canopies of shade cloth. Perennials and annuals will usually be in separate areas. If most of the plants you pick out are shades of green, look for annual flowers to plant among perennials to add a bit of color.

Bearded iris

Coral bells

Columbine

Super Shade Perennials

5 Rake some mulch around the newly added perennials. Shredded hardwood bark mulch and composted leaf mulch are both dark brown, provide nutrients, keep moisture in the soil, and provide a finished look to the garden bed. Be careful not to mound mulch around the plant stems.

6 After mulching, water the plants. Count to ten while watering each plant, and then repeat the process. Shade gardens, even newly planted ones, need less water than sun gardens because the water evaporates less quickly. You should water new plants two or three times a week for the first month, and once or twice a week after that for the first year.

Success Tip

You will read, repeatedly, in this book to select and plant plants with one another that share the same water needs. That's because you can't easily change the amount of water given to plants planted next to one another.

Fern

Camellia

Azalea

How to Grow Flowering Bulbs

Flowering bulbs bloom for only a short period—one to two weeks per plant—but their intense color and unique flower forms are unmatched by other plants in the garden. It's worth the time to make room for annual and perennial, spring- or summer- flowering bulbs in the garden. To make the biggest splash with your bulb display, plant in groups of ten or more. One tulip doesn't make a big impact, but one hundred tulips create a sight your neighbors will ask you about. Here's how to plant and grow bulbs easily.

What You'll Need

- ☐ Trowel or soil knife
- ☐ Bulbs
- ☐ Watering can
- ☐ Rake
- ☐ Flower pot
- ☐ Potting soil
- ☐ Ground cayenne pepper

Instant Green Thumb

There are three things you need to remember to grow bulbs successfully.

- Place the bulbs in the planting holes with the pointy ends up.

- Water flowering bulbs once a week unless the ground is frozen.

- Don't cut off the bulb leaves until they've turned completely yellow or brown.

How to Plant Bulbs Individually

1 Plant larger bulbs (bulbs the size of your closed fist) in individual holes. Use a trowel or soil knife to dig a hole that is four times as deep as the height of the bulb.

2 Place the bulb in the hole with the pointed end up. You don't need to put bonemeal or bloodmeal in the hole. In fact, bonemeal acts like a homing beacon to squirrels that would like nothing better than to dig up the bulbs so skip it.

3 If you have several bulbs to plant, you'll be done faster (and you won't forget where you've already planted) if you set the bulbs out first, then plant each one. Don't be afraid to really pack the bulbs into the planting area. Dig the holes, plant them, cover the holes with soil, and top with mulch.

4 After planting all of the bulbs, give them a drink. Count to ten while watering each bulb area. Spring-flowering bulbs need to grow roots before the ground freezes, so don't plant and forget them. Make sure to water once a week until the ground freezes.

How to Plant Large Groups of Bulbs

You don't have to dig individual holes if you're planting a large number of bulbs in one, concentrated area. Use this technique for filling areas bigger than a one-foot by one-foot square with bulbs.

1 First scrape the mulch away from the planting area. Then remove the soil from the planting area to make a trench or hole that is the depth of four to six times the height of the bulbs you're planting.

2 Then, set the bulbs in the planting area. For a natural look, mix several types of bulbs together in a bucket and then scatter them on the ground. Fix the bulbs so the pointy end is up.

Parrot tulip

3 Sprinkle ground cayenne pepper on the bulbs to keep the squirrels from eating the bulbs. (They don't like the taste of the pepper.) If you have serious problems with creatures digging up bulbs, consider making a makeshift cage out of chicken wire. Plant the bulbs in the cage and bury it.

4 Cover the bulbs with soil. You'll want to cover them with enough soil so that the bulbs are buried at least four to six times their height. If you don't feel like digging, you don't have to. Scatter the bulbs and cover them with soil at least four to six times as deep as the bulbs are tall. Your flower bed will be slightly taller in the spring, but you'll have saved yourself a lot of work!

5 Use a shrub rake or hard rake to spread mulch over the planting area for a finishing touch. You can use the same mulch that you use in the rest of the planting bed for this step. Remember to water the bulbs after you're done planting them.

How to Plant Bulb Containers

Create beautiful blooming spring containers that look like they were designed by a pro. Follow these tips.

1 Use a plastic container (so it won't crack during the winter), and fill it about one-third full with potting soil. Use potting soil, which is a lightweight mix made especially for container gardens.

2 Next, place the bulbs in the pot, pointy end up. Really pack the bulbs into the container. You can place the bulbs so they're almost touching one another. A secret of the pros: more bulbs equals more excitement. You can also plant a mixture of bulbs that bloom at different times to extend the flower show on your front porch.

3 Then, add potting soil to the container so that it is two-thirds to three-fourths full of potting soil. This will ensure that the bulbs are deep enough. Leave room in the container to add more potting soil and annual flowers on top.

4 Plant cool-weather annuals on top of the bulbs. Pansies and flowering kale are the most cold-tolerant, but snapdragons and calendula are good choices for warmer climates as well. You can also plant perennials like coral bells on top of the bulbs. Plant the annuals and perennials close together in the pot. This container uses twelve pansy plants.

5 Fill in around the flowering annuals with more potting soil, and leave one-half to one inch between the top of the soil and the rim of the container so that the soil doesn't wash out when you water the plants.

6 Last, water the container. Make sure to water the flowers at least once a week throughout the winter, unless the soil in the pot is frozen solid. Leave the flower pot outside all winter. While the bulbs are "chilling," you can enjoy the flowering annuals. In the spring, the bulbs will grow up through the annual flowers.

Success Tip

Spring-flowering bulbs need a "chilling period" to bloom well in the spring. If you live in the South, you can still enjoy spring-flowering bulbs, but you'll need to purchase bulbs that are marked as "pre-chilled."

| Crocosmia | Dahlia | Lily of the Nile | Gladiola | Asiatic lily |

Just Grow With It!

You can enjoy bulbs in your garden throughout the growing season. Plant a variety of bulbs that bloom at different times to enjoy endless color.

Spring Bulbs

Plant spring-flowering bulbs in the fall when the leaves are falling off the trees.

- Peony
- Tulip
- Daffodil
- Crocus
- Hyacinth
- Grape hyacinth
- Siberian iris
- Bearded iris
- Anemone
- Ranunculus
- Snowdrops
- Spanish bluebell

Summer Bulbs

Plant summer-blooming bulbs in the spring right after tulips have finished flowering.

- Asiatic lily
- Crocosmia
- Red hot poker
- Canna
- Ginger lily
- Lily of the Nile
- Caladium (annual)
- Gladiola (annual)
- Pineapple lily
- Gloriosa lily
- Tuberous begonia
- Elephant ear

| Anemone | Daffodil | Allium | Spanish bluebell | Tulip |

Spring Bulbs

How to Fix Flower Problems

Good plant care techniques go a long way toward preventing problems because healthy plants can fight off many problems on their own. It's important not to give plants more fertilizer than they need—perennials rarely need to be fed, and annuals only need to be fertilized once a month. If the plant leaves look yellow or purple, they might not be receiving enough of the right food because the soil pH is off, so check the pH, and if it isn't between 5.5 to 7.0, correct it. Other problems require intervention. Here's how to fix common flower problems.

What You'll Need

- Nitrile gloves
- Diatomaceous earth
- Deer repellent
- Beer
- Jar lid or butter lid
- Fungicide in spray bottle
- Ground cayenne pepper

Instant Green Thumb

Because there are so many insects, bacteria, fungi, and other creatures in the air, water, and soil, it's impossible to grow a pest-free garden, nor would you want to. Insects are an important food source for birds. And that caterpillar chewing on the fennel in your vegetable garden? It's probably a swallowtail butterfly caterpillar. Before treating for pests, decide what level of damage you're willing to tolerate. You might not have to do anything at all.

Problems and Solutions

Deer Damage

Deer eat the tender growth off of plants (tulip flowers, hosta leaves, rose petals), causing damage. They do tend to leave thorny, spiky, or smelly foliage and flowers alone.

One line of defense against deer is to build a tall fence—at least 10 feet. That's not practical for larger gardens. An alternative is to plant things that deer don't like to eat. Daffodils and grape hyacinth are go-to choices for deer-resistant bulbs.

You can also spray plants with deer repellent. In order for repellent to be effective, you should change the brand of repellent every six months or the deer will get used to it.

Slugs

Use beer traps or diatomaceous earth to prevent slugs from damaging your plants. To make a beer trap, put a shallow jar or butter lid on the ground next to the afflicted plant. Fill the trap with beer to catch the slugs. Diatomaceous earth is made from fossilized remains of sea creatures. It is a fine powder that you can sprinkle on the soil around the plant stems to act as a barrier to prevent slugs from eating the plants. Slugs don't like the sharp edges of diatomaceous earth.

Japanese Beetles

Almost every flowering plant or vegetable is fair game for Japanese beetles. They're not picky eaters. The best way to control Japanese beetles is to use milky spore to kill their immature form—grubs that live in the lawn and soil. Grubs need to be eating their way through warm soil for milky spore to work. Early fall is the best time to spread milky spore on the lawn according to package instructions.

Powdery Mildew

Powdery mildew strikes plants during hot, dry, humid weather (primarily during humid summers with little rain). This disease makes plants look like someone shook a flour sifter over them. There are plants that are resistant to powdery mildew. Fungicides available from garden centers and home-improvement stores can control powdery mildew. Never compost plant parts that have been infected with powdery mildew—throw them away.

Botrytis (Gray Mold)

If your flower looks like it was just dipped in a bucket of gray dryer lint while wet, it has botrytis. If only some parts of the plants are affected, cut off the diseased parts and throw them away. (Do not compost them.) You can also spray plants with fungicides available at garden centers and home-improvement stores. Always read the labels when spraying fungicides.

Part Six: Vegetables

You will never forget the first time you pick a vegetable that you grew yourself. Tomatoes fresh from the vine are sweeter, juicier, and more flavorful than anything you can buy at the grocery store. Lettuce cut right from the garden and tossed with a light vinaigrette is delicate and tender instead of tough. Summer squash that you grow yourself is crunchy and not rubbery. You just can't beat homegrown vegetables.

Additionally, when you grow your own food, you control how pests are dealt with and the way the plants are fed. Growing your own gives you more control over what you eat. In this part, you'll learn how to select, grow, and harvest your own vegetables.

Know the Lingo

Look up the definitions of these terms in the glossary before reading through this part, and you'll have a leg up on your learning!

- Acidic soil
- Alkaline soil
- Beneficial insect
- Bolting
- Cool-season vegetable
- Cover crop
- Granular fertilizer
- Hardening off
- Heirloom
- Hybrid
- Irrigation
- Jute twine
- Liquid fertilizer
- Pinch
- Side dress
- Warm-season vegetable

How to Plant Warm-Season Vegetables

When you think "vegetable gardening," you're probably picturing yourself biting into a big, juicy tomato. In that case, you're thinking about summer and warm-season vegetables. During the summer, or when nighttime temperatures are at least 60 degrees or higher, you can grow mouth-watering favorites, such as tomatoes, basil, peppers, squash, okra, green beans, corn, and eggplants. Here's how to plant your warm-season vegetables.

What You'll Need

- [ ] Compost
- [ ] Plant starts (transplants)
- [ ] Seeds
- [ ] Seed starting mix
- [ ] Trowel or hoe
- [ ] Hose and watering wand
- [ ] Wheat straw or grass clippings

Instant Green Thumb

Lusting after your neighbors' luscious tomatoes? They have a secret—they plant their tomatoes deep. Most plants need to be planted with the soil level in the pot the same depth as the soil level around the plant. Not tomatoes. Pinch off all but the top two sets of tomato leaves, and bury the tomato all the way up to the (now) bottom set of leaves.

Step-by-Step

1 Prepare the planting area by adding compost. You can buy bagged compost at garden centers and home-improvement stores. Use a hard rake or 4 tine claw to incorporate the compost into a prepared vegetable bed.

2 Set out your plants. It is always tempting to cram a lot of vegetable plants into a small space, especially when they're little transplants. Resist that urge! Follow instructions on the package about spacing. You can always thin seeds, but transplants are too expensive to throw away.

Just Grow With It!

Most warm-season vegetables are easiest to grow from transplants, but some picky plants prefer not to be moved, so plant seeds of those plants (beans, squash, and melons) directly into the garden. Sow seeds when nighttime temperatures have reached at least 65 degrees. Use your trowel or hoe to dig a row. Plant two seeds per grouping according to package instructions, and cover with one-half inch of soil.

3 Plant tomatoes deep and plant everything else so that the plant's rootball matches the soil level surrounding the planting hole. You don't need to put fertilizer in the planting hole.

4 Spread mulch around the plants. Mulch is just as important in vegetable gardens as it is in flower gardens because it helps keep water in the soil, moderates the soil temperature, and prevents weeds from sprouting. Use wheat straw or grass clippings in vegetable gardens. Warm-season veggies like it hot. If you don't have straw or grass clippings, you can actually use black plastic as a "mulch." It will trap the heat in the soil.

Success Tip

There's another way to keep weeds from sprouting in the vegetable garden: you can use pre-emergent herbicide. Weed and feed products marked for vegetables have a combination of fertilizer and weed preventer. Corn gluten (usually marked as the "organic weed preventer") is now available for vegetable gardens as well.

Wait until your vegetable plants have been growing for at least two weeks before spreading these weed preventers.

Tomato

Red bell pepper

Warm-Season Vegetables

5 Place stakes and supports around newly planted vegetables right after you plant them. Tomatoes have brittle stems, so it is difficult to maneuver them into cages after they've started growing. Tomato cages are inexpensive and the best support for tomato plants.

6 Water the plants by directing the watering wand or hose nozzle at the base of the plant. Count to ten while watering each plant and then go back and repeat the process. If you have the time and money, put soaker hoses around your vegetable garden beds. It will be much easier to water—you can just turn on the hoses and let them run for a while while you do something else.

Success Tip

It will take your vegetables a few weeks to grow new roots in the vegetable garden bed. During that time, it is crucial to water the plants daily, or if it is really hot (above 85 degrees), twice a day—in the morning and the evening.

Vegetables without enough water develop problems and have trouble fighting off pests and diseases.

Summer squash

Winter squash

How to Plant Cool-Season Vegetables

Vegetable gardening doesn't end when summer fades and cool temperatures return. Fall and spring are second seasons for gardeners. Cool-weather vegetables grow fast, and most of them are easy to start from seed right in the garden. Here's how to get more out of your vegetable gardens by growing greens, broccoli, cabbage, and cover crops from seeds or from transplants.

What You'll Need

- ☐ Compost
- ☐ Vegetable seeds
- ☐ Vegetable transplants
- ☐ Trowel
- ☐ Plant tags
- ☐ Pencil
- ☐ Seed starting mix
- ☐ Sand
- ☐ 4 tine claw

Instant Green Thumb

Never plant vegetables from the cabbage family in the same place more frequently than every other year. Broccoli, cauliflower, kale, Brussels sprouts, cabbage, and collards are all in the cabbage family, and they are highly susceptible to several plant diseases that live in the soil. Once the plants are affected, there's nothing you can do but pull them up. Rotating planting locations of these veggies helps prevent problems.

Planting Cool-Season Transplants

1 Before planting anything in the garden, get some worm castings (worm poop), mushroom compost, or composted cow manure to rake into the soil. Spread a one-inch layer on top of the soil and use a 4 tine claw to work it in.

2 Once the soil is prepared, set out the plants according to spacing instructions on the plant tag. Broccoli, cabbage, and kale plants need 12 to 18 inches of space between them. Lettuce only needs 8 inches of space between plants.

Broccoli   *Carrot*   *Radish*   *Swiss chard*

3 After you've planted everything, water each plant by placing the water breaker on the hose at the base of each plant and counting to ten. To make quick work of watering, put a soaker hose around your plants to water them. You can snake the hose in and out of rows and use wire pins called sod staples to hold down the hose. If the hose is in the middle of two rows, the water from it will reach plants on each side of the hose.

4 Spread mulch around the vegetable transplants. If you live in a warmer area, this will help keep water in the soil during those hot, Indian summer fall days. In cooler areas, the mulch acts to insulate the vegetables, helping them stay warmer longer into the fall. Straw is good for vegetable gardens because it is lightweight. Most garden centers and home-improvement stores sell bales of wheat straw. Just ask for it if you don't see it.

Kale   *Cauliflower*   *Cabbage*

Planting Cool-Season Root Vegetables

1 Root vegetables, such as carrots, parsnips, radishes, turnips, and beets, are easy to grow from seed, as long as you have relatively loose, crumbly soil. If there are lots of rocks in your soil, pick them out before planting. If, when your soil is wet, a handful of it feels sticky like pottery clay, mix some sand and compost into the soil to loosen it up.

2 Check the soil pH before planting seeds. If it is lower than 6.0, sprinkle garden lime on the soil according to the package instructions and rake it in. Then, sow the seeds in garden rows according to package spacing instructions, and cover the seeds by sprinkling one-fourth inch of seed starting mix on top of them. Water the seeds daily until they sprout. Water two or three times a week after that.

Planting a Salad Bowl

This is a fun project that gives you lettuce longer. The bowl is portable, so you can move it around on colder or warmer days to give the lettuce the conditions it needs to grow.

1 Purchase wide, shallow pots to plant salad bowls, or, if you have an old plastic salad bowl, you can drill holes in the bottom and plant it. Fill the bowl about halfway with potting soil.

2 Plant the lettuce bowl with lettuce transplants. For extra taste, plant some bunching onions in the center of the bowl and a dill plant or two on the edges. Fill in around the plants with potting soil and water the plants. On hot days, move the bowl into some shade. On cool days, move the bowl into the sun. If temperatures are forecast to drop below freezing, bring the bowl into the garage.

Planting Cover Crops

You can take advantage of cover crops, even as a beginning gardener. Cover crops are sometimes called "green manure," because after you let them grow for a few months, you will cut them down and turn them into the soil to add nutrients to the garden. Annual ryegrass, peas, clover, and wheat are all good winter cover crops that prevent soil from washing away during the winter.

1 If you buy cover crop seeds in individual packages (particularly peas), instead of by the pound, dump all of the seed packages into a big bowl to save time opening packages later. Planting will go faster!

2 Use a hoe to dig rows that are six inches apart. Then, plant the seeds and cover them with one inch of soil. Cover cropping works best if you can plant a large section of the garden or an entire 4x4 raised bed with the same type of seeds. Water the seeds daily until they sprout, then water every four or five days.

Just Grow With It!

Cool-season vegetables are just that—they thrive in cool weather. Some tolerate heat (temperatures above 80 degrees) better than others, and some won't sprout unless the soil temperature has started to drop. For success with cool-season vegetables, plant a mixture of seeds and transplants once the daytime air temperatures are consistently in the low 70s.

Easy Seeds
- Carrot
- Radish
- Turnip
- Lettuce
- Beet
- Bunching onion
- Leek
- Pea

Start With Transplants
- Broccoli
- Cabbage
- Cauliflower
- Kale
- Swiss chard
- Brussels sprouts
- Collard greens

How to Care for Vegetables

Picking and eating a ripe tomato straight off the vine is nothing short of a miracle. The idea of growing your own is fun and functional, especially with rising food prices and food safety scares. Vegetables are a bit more particular than perennials, trees, and shrubs. They also have a job to do, and they need support to do it. Plenty of food, water, and TLC go into home garden vegetables. Here's how to keep your plants perky and producing all season long.

What You'll Need

- ☐ Plant stakes
- ☐ Tomato cages
- ☐ Fertilizer (liquid or granular)
- ☐ Hose and watering wand
- ☐ Twine
- ☐ Scissors
- ☐ Hand pruners

Instant Green Thumb

The secret to successful vegetable gardening is actually in the flowers. That's right: planting flowers with your vegetables will lure pollinators, deter pests, and encourage visits from beneficial insects.

Make room in the vegetable garden for these herbs and flowers: marigolds, nasturtium, bee balm, dill, sage, borage, chamomile, fennel, and hyssop. You can also leave some lettuce and radishes to bolt (flower). Pollinators love their small, sweet-smelling flowers.

Vegetable Care Techniques

Supporting

Many vegetables need support to grow upright and produce food. Peppers and eggplants do well when individually staked. Place the stake in the ground next to the plant stem and loosely tie the stem to the stake. Tomatoes, cucumbers, and pole beans prefer to climb up and through trellises and cages.

Watering

Drip irrigation is the way to go if you can. Using soaker hoses is an easy way to accomplish this. If you are hand-watering, water deeply at the base of the plant. (Measure your time by counting to ten while watering each plant.) Peppers are the only vegetables that can dry out a bit without suffering.

When to Pick Vegetables

Some vegetables turn a different color when they're ripe—tomatoes and some peppers, for example. Some vegetables don't change color (eggplants, green peppers). Others should be picked when the flower has just fallen off the end of the vegetable (peas and zucchini). Look on the plant tag for information about the eventual size of the vegetable and use it as a guide for harvesting.

Greens like lettuce, collards, kale, Swiss chard, and spinach don't change colors when they're ripe. You can harvest everything but lettuce by picking the lowest leaves on the plant. (Don't pinch off the growing tip of these plants, or you'll stop getting leaves.) "Cut and come again" lettuce (labeled that way on the package) can be sheared off with garden scissors. It will resprout to give you more tasty salads.

Mulching

Just as in the flower garden, mulch is an integral part of the vegetable garden. Use grass clippings, shredded newspapers, or wheat straw to mulch vegetables. The mulch helps keep plant roots cool and moist and adds organic matter (which feeds the plants and helps keep water in the soil). These mulches also add nutrients to the soil as they break down. If you've never used mulch in the vegetable garden before, you'll be amazed at how helpful it is for growing vegetables.

Feeding

Plants are what they eat, and they eat a lot. There are two commonly used types of vegetable fertilizers: liquid and slow release. "Side dress" vegetables by spreading slow-release fertilizer around the plants. Rake the fertilizer lightly into the soil. When feeding with slow-release fertilizer, you'll only need to feed once a month to every few months. (Read the package label for directions.) Liquid fertilizers are watered into the soil and generally have to be reapplied every two to three weeks.

Pruning/Pinching

Some plants need more pruning and pinching than others. Remove the flowers from all herb plants (basil, sage, oregano, and so forth) in order to keep them producing fragrant leaves full of essential oils. Pinch suckers from tomato and pepper plants. (Suckers are extra branches that sprout from the spot between the main stem and main side branches.) The fewer main stems and branches on a tomato or pepper plant, the larger the fruits.

Harvesting

Pick vegetables when they're ripe to keep the plants producing. Tomatoes, peppers, and eggplants all turn colors when they're ready. (The size and color depends on the variety.) Pick zucchini when the flower on the end of the fruit just starts to wither. Pole beans, snap peas, and string beans are ready to harvest while they're still young and tender. English peas should be fat and ready to burst before picking. Lettuce, kale, Swiss chard, and other greens can be picked from the outside, in, until they start to flower. Broccoli, cauliflower, and cabbages should be picked when they still look "tight."

Just Grow With It!

If you're interested in growing vegetables, you've probably heard about raised bed gardening. So what's the fuss all about? Raised bed gardening makes growing vegetables much easier for people with limited space or time, mobility challenges, and polluted soils. By gardening in raised beds, you can grow more food in less space, more easily control the soil and growing conditions, and contend with fewer weed problems.

Benefits of raised bed gardening

- Easy to assemble
- Elevated gardening area
- Less soil compaction
- Fewer problems with slugs and underground pests
- More control over the soil quality

Challenges of raised bed gardening

- Difficult to move/disassemble
- High startup costs (soil + raised bed kit = $$)
- Limited space for growing

Is raised bed gardening for you? It does make vegetable gardening easier, especially for new gardeners, if the startup costs aren't a problem.

How to Fix Vegetable Problems

There is no group of plants more afflicted with pests and problems than vegetables. Centuries of breeding plants for their juicy fruit or tender leaves has made vegetables as appetizing to pests as they are to people. There are some techniques you can use to recognize pests and problems when you see them and to treat the problems properly. Here's how to take care of vegetable problems.

What You'll Need

- [ ] Nitrile gloves
- [ ] Dust mask
- [ ] Long-sleeved shirt
- [ ] Long pants
- [ ] Garden hose
- [ ] Spray nozzle
- [ ] Flower seeds
- [ ] Insecticidal soap
- [ ] Soapy water in a bucket
- [ ] Insect dust
- [ ] Soaker hose

Instant Green Thumb

Plant tags have information about disease resistance. Buy resistant varieties for fewer problems. Look for these letters:

- N: resistant to nematodes
- V: resistant to verticillium wilt
- T or TMV: resistant to tobacco mosaic virus
- TSWV: resistant to tobacco spotted wilt virus
- PMR: resistant to powdery mildew

Problems and Solutions

Drought

Plants experiencing drought stop growing, and their leaves curl up to reduce water loss. During extremely dry periods (which for vegetables can be two or more weeks without rain), use soaker hoses around vegetables to keep moisture levels consistent.

Blossom End Rot

Low calcium levels in the soil and uneven soil moisture both cause blossom end rot in peppers and tomatoes. To correct this problem in new fruits (you can't fix tomatoes that already have the problem), use soaker hoses around plants to keep the soil evenly moist. If the soil pH is less than 6.5, add garden lime.

Just Grow With It!

Flowers and vegetables are best friends in the garden. Flowers lure pollinators like bees, birds, and butterflies. Vegetable plants need pollinators to produce large, juicy tomatoes, squash, eggplants, peppers, and more. Marigold and nasturtium flowers help vegetables by discouraging pest insects (marigolds) or trapping pest insects (nasturtiums). Make room for flowers next to vegetables.

Cracking Fruit

Tomatoes are the vegetable most likely to have cracking problems. Two conditions that cause tomatoes to crack are uneven moisture and fast growth. Soaker hoses really are a gardener's best helper. Water with the hoses for an hour in the morning and again in the evening. To avoid fast growth that causes cracks, use a low-Nitrogen fertilizer. Look on the fertilizer label; the first number of the analysis should be zero (as in 0-5-5).

Aphids

Ladybug larvae (baby ladybugs) like to eat aphids, so encourage ladybugs to live in your garden. If you see aphids before there are so many that they're completely covering the entire plant, you can spray them off with a hard stream of water from a "water gun" type of nozzle. The next line of defense is insecticidal soap. Because aphids have soft bodies, the soap dries them out. Read the soap label for correct spraying instructions.

Squash Bugs

Squash bugs suck the juice out of plant leaves and stems, which causes the leaves to turn brown and die. These bugs are also vectors (which means they transmit) for the Yellow Vine Decline disease that causes squashes and pumpkins to wilt and die. As soon as you see the eggs (they look like very small red Tic-Tacs) on the underside of the leaves, pick them off. If you see the bugs (pictured), use Sevin dust. Always wear a dust mask, gloves, and long sleeves when dusting with Sevin.

Squash Vine Borer Moth and Caterpillar

This moth kills squashes, cucumbers, and melons. The adult moth looks like a wasp. From late May to late June, the moths emerge from underground cocoons and lay eggs at the base of squash plants. The borer worms hatch and burrow into the squash stems, causing the plants to wilt. The best way for beginning gardeners to control borers is to plant squash in July after the moths have stopped laying eggs.

Cabbage White Butterfly

Cabbage white butterflies are as common as they are pretty, which is to say, very. The butterflies lay eggs that hatch into large, fat cabbage worms that eat cabbage plants from the bottom, up. To control damage from cabbage worms, notice if there are cabbage whites near your vegetables and start checking the undersides of cabbage plant leaves for caterpillars. Pick off the caterpillars and drop them in buckets of soapy water to kill them.

Tomato Hornworm

There is no mistaking a tomato hornworm. It is the largest, fattest caterpillar you'll see in the garden. Hornworms are as big as your thumb, and they do have horns. Sometimes you'll see parasitic wasps covering the hornworms (pictured). When you see hornworms, put on gloves and pick them off the plants. Drop them in soapy water to kill them before they eat your tomato plants to the ground.

Chipmunks

The most frustrating part of having chipmunks visit the garden is that they'll take a bite or two out of your tomatoes and then leave them on the vine to rot. You can try trapping chipmunks with catch-and-release traps, but you have to let them out in your yard, so that's pointless. Instead, spray plants with repellents or sprinkle ground red cayenne pepper on plants (and flowers) to keep chipmunks from nibbling.

Slugs

Most people think that slugs only enjoy eating leaves. Not true! They also chomp on vegetables. Prevent slugs from taking over by setting beer traps around your plants. Fill a shallow jar lid with beer and put it on the ground near the plant stem. The slugs will be attracted to the beer and drown. You can also sprinkle diatomaceous earth around the plant stems to act as a barrier to slugs. Diatomaceous earth is ground up fossilized sea creatures. It has sharp edges, which slugs will avoid.

Part Seven: Finishing Touches

Now that you've mastered the basics, you're ready to learn how to put the final "shine" on your garden with these finishing touches. The techniques in this part will help you clean up landscape beds, garden in problem areas, and spiff up porches and patios with extra color.

One of the most fun gardening techniques, planting a container garden, is also part of the "Finishing Touches." Container gardens are places for you to let your creativity run wild, and you'll find plenty of ideas to help you get started.

The information in this book is, really, just the beginning for you. Reading through this book, you'll learn how to start caring for your garden. from this point, forward, you'll keep adding to your knowledge base. In gardening, there's nothing like experience!

Know the Lingo

Look up the definitions of these terms in the glossary before reading through this part, and you'll have a leg up on your learning!

- Blower
- Container
- Container garden
- Deadhead
- Hard rake

- Liquid fertilizer
- Mulch
- Potting soil
- Power edger
- Shop broom

- Shovel
- Shrub rake
- Snips
- Spade
- Wood chips

How to Mulch and Edge Landscape Beds

Edging a landscape bed is the best way to keep mulch and water from spilling out onto the sidewalk, driveway, or yard while you're watering or during a hard rain. The water or mulch will get caught in the trench made when you edge. You can edge with a power edger, but you can also edge with just a sharp spade. After edging, add mulch. Mulch is the finishing touch for every garden or landscape bed. Not only does mulch look pretty, it also helps keep weeds from sprouting, holds water in the soil, cools plant roots, and adds nutrients to the soil.

What You'll Need

- ☐ Mulch
- ☐ Hard rake
- ☐ Pitchfork
- ☐ Sharpened spade
- ☐ Wheelbarrow
- ☐ Pre-emergent herbicide
- ☐ Shop broom
- ☐ Garden gloves

Instant Green Thumb

Never sweep yard clippings or yard waste into the street, because it will clog storm drains. Clogged storm drains cause flooding in towns and cities. Yard debris can also clog creeks and rivers and cause flooding.

By adding your debris to your compost pile, or taking it to a dropoff location, you'll protect yourself and your neighbors from problems caused by this type of waste.

How to Edge Landscape Beds

1 With your sharpened spade, stand on the outside of your garden or landscape bed and hold the spade at the edge of the bed at a 90-degree angle with the spade handle leaning back into the bed. Chop an angle with the spade along the entire bed. During this step, you'll remove soil or sod clumps from the edge of the bed.

2 Use a shop broom or pitchfork to clean up. Pick up grass clumps and compost them. If you're edging along a hard surface, use a shop broom to sweep the soil into a dust pan (put the soil in the compost pile), or to push back the soil into the bed, away from the newly cut edge.

How to Add Wood Mulch to Landscape Beds

1 Before adding any mulch, spread a pre-emergent herbicide. There are organic and conventional choices for pre-emergents. Pre-emergents work by preventing weed seeds from sprouting. You'll save yourself a lot of time and backaches if you use a pre-emergent. (However, if you have an area where you like to let plants go to seed, and you leave the seeds to resprout, *don't* use pre-emergent.)

2 Next, add the mulch by creating little piles around your landscape beds. You can buy mulch two ways: in bags or in bulk. Most home-improvement stores sell bagged mulch, and they'll probably have several different brands of the same type of mulch. Some home-improvement stores and garden centers sell bulk mulch. To buy bulk mulch, you usually need a truck so that you can bring home a big load. If you're buying more than three cubic yards of mulch, you will want to consider delivery. A pitchfork and wheelbarrow are handy for moving bulk mulch.

3 Use a hard rake or a 4 tine claw to rake the mulch around the bed. Start raking from either the back or one side of the bed so that you can leave "fluffy" mulch behind you. You will want to put mulch across the entire bed, at least three inches deep.

4 After spreading the mulch in the landscape bed, pull the mulch slightly away from plant stems and leaves. Mulch is usually warm and moist—the perfect environment for bacteria and fungi to live and thrive. These microorganisms can rot your plant stems, so leave a little breathing room between the mulch and plants.

Success Tip

Whether you buy bulk or bagged mulch, if you can't spread it for several days or weeks, cover it with a tarp to keep the rain out. Wet mulch is three or four times heavier to lift than dry mulch.

How to Spread Pine Straw Mulch

Pine straw mulch is particularly common in the Southeast, where longleaf, loblolly, and slash pines grow natively. There's a trick to spreading this type of mulch without making a mess. Here's how.

1 Buy the mulch. Pine straw is sold in bales, just like hay. Bales can be prickly, and spiders and other insects like to hang out in pine straw, so use gloves when handling the bales. Look for bales that don't appear to have a lot of other material in them—cones, twigs, or pieces of ferns. Pine straw is raked and baled from yards and commercial forests, and sometimes it comes with hitchhiking plants or weeds. Nutsedge is one type of weed that tends to come along, so if you can, put down a pre-emergent herbicide before using pine straw. If you need to control nutsedge that is already sprouting, Image® is the best chemical product to use—it is virtually the only thing that will kill nutsedge.

2 To add the pine straw to the landscape, simply snip the twine holding a bale together, and the bale will break apart into clumps called "flakes." Sprinkle the flakes around the landscape bed or trees, being careful to keep the straw near the ground. If you fling pine straw around above your waist, you'll end up with needles hanging all over your shrubs, and that's annoying to clean up!

3 The newly spread straw will be fluffy, and it will most likely escape the landscape beds. To tidy up the beds, you'll want to rake and tuck the straw to keep it in place. Using a hard rake, pull the straw into the edge of the landscape bed. Step on the straw on top of the rake, and then, leaving your foot where it is, pull the rake out. This bunches up the straw at the edge of the bed.

4 To tuck the straw, after raking, plunge a sharpened spade or shovel into the ground about one inch inside the landscape bed. This will trap the edge of the straw in the soil, and will keep it from blowing out of the bed. You can use a chopping motion to do this.

How Much Mulch?

To calculate the amount of mulch you need, multiply the length and width of the area (in feet) that you're mulching. Then multiply by .25. That will give you the number of cubic feet of mulch you need. (Remember, 3 cubic feet=1 cubic yard.) Mulch is sold by the cubic foot (marked on the bag) and cubic yards (when you buy in bulk). You can also find "mulch calculators" online. These allow you to put in the size of area you're mulching and select the depth of mulch you'd like, and the calculator will tell you how much mulch to buy.

Just Grow With It!

If the municipality where you live picks up yard debris, you might wonder if you should use free mulch your city or county makes from the debris. The answer is "maybe."

Yes: Use free mulch made from yard debris if you want to "sheet compost" to enlarge your vegetable garden. To sheet compost, spread layers of newspaper across the grass, cover them with the free mulch, top with shredded leaves or grass clippings, and finish with the addition of compost or topsoil. In other words, sheet composting is not a delicate process, so it doesn't matter if you start with coarse mulch. You can also use this coarse, fresh mulch for driveways, pathways, and "the back forty."

No: Don't use coarse, fresh wood chip mulch in landscape beds or already-producing vegetable gardens. Usually this mulch is full of junk (sometimes trash), a variety of materials, and large twigs; it needs time to decompose before it's "ready for its closeup."

Maybe: Before using any mulch from your municipality, check to make sure that they don't include shavings or ground up pieces from construction sites, which might contain pressure-treated wood. Pressure-treated wood has chemicals that make it unsuitable for garden use.

Mulching Near Drainage Areas

Strike a happy medium between mulched areas, grass, and drainage pipes. If a drainage pipe lets out into a landscape bed, use a little bit of gravel right by the output area. The gravel will slow the flow of water, stop the mulch from washing out of the bed, and will keep soil in the lawn from washing away.

How to Landscape Wet Areas

What is considered a "wet area" of the yard? If you have a space in your yard or garden that is always moist, never dries out, or always feels wet if you stick your finger in the soil, that's a "wet area." Different from a pond (which is sopping wet all of the time) or a drainage swale (which is wet for a day or two after a storm), a wet area of the yard is always damp like a sponge that hasn't been wrung out. Here's how to turn your wet area into a beautiful garden.

What You'll Need

- [ ] Plants
- [ ] Mulch
- [ ] Spade or shovel

Instant Green Thumb

Have you heard of rain gardens? These are areas that are wet for 24 to 48 hours after collecting water from gutters, sidewalks, and driveways after storms. Rain gardens help clean stormwater by allowing the water to slowly soak into the ground instead of running into drains. Plants in rain gardens have to tolerate both wet and dry conditions.

If you have an area of the yard that collects water from a downspout, consider planting a rain garden to spruce up your yard and help the environment.

Tips for Planting Wet Areas

Plant Selection Is Key

You can grow a beautiful garden in the wettest, swampiest part of your yard if you choose the right plants. When shopping for plants, look at the plant tags for indicators like water use equals high, or soil conditions equal moist.

Use Mulch but Don't Add to the Soil

The beauty of selecting the right plants, plants that like wet feet, is that you don't need to do *anything* to the soil. Plant the plants, and add shredded hardwood mulch around them (pull the mulch slightly away from the plant stems).

Sun Plants for Wet Areas

Hardy hibiscus   *Canna*   *Umbrella plant*   *Louisiana iris*   *Amsonia*

Just Grow With It!

Damp areas of the yard don't have to be swampy expanses of half-dead grass. Instead of fighting the water, embrace it by planting these plants that thrive in wet conditions. Read the plant tags for water and sun requirements, and make sure that you select plants for the amount of sun in your yard: sun, shade, or partial sun/shade.

Sun Plants for Wet Areas

- Hardy hibiscus
- Swamp sunflower
- Amsonia
- Canna lily
- Ginger lily
- Louisiana iris
- Umbrella plant
- New England aster
- Beautyberry
- Virginia sweetspire
- Cranberry viburnum

Shade Plants for Wet Areas

- Goatsbeard
- Leopard plant
- Lady's mantle
- Astilbe
- Siberian bugloss
- Elephant ear
- Ajuga
- Lirope
- Painted fern
- Cardinal flower
- Turtlehead

Goatsbeard   *Leopard plant*   *Lady's mantle*   *Siberian bugloss*   *Elephant ear*

Shade Plants for Wet Areas

How to Garden in Narrow Spaces

Modern houses are built on smaller lots with smaller yards, with many on zero lot lines (no space between the house and the edge of the lot). All isn't lost if you have a yard the size of a postage stamp or a narrow patio with tiny planting beds around it. There are some tricks to gardening in narrow spaces while still creating a gorgeous outdoor oasis. Here's how to garden in narrow spaces.

What You'll Need

- ☐ Trellis
- ☐ Twine
- ☐ Vines
- ☐ Hanging baskets
- ☐ Climbing plants

Instant Green Thumb

You can find many of your favorite plants in columnar (tall and narrow) varieties. Look for these plants when shopping for your narrow garden:

- 🌿 'Crimson Sentry' maple
- 🌿 Columnar hornbeam
- 🌿 'Cleveland Select' pear
- 🌿 'Graham Blandy' boxwood
- 🌿 'Sky Pencil' holly
- 🌿 'Skyrocket' juniper

Landscaping Narrow Spaces

Limit Your Plant Picks

In narrow landscape beds, there usually isn't room for more than two rows of plants. To make the narrow garden look interesting, but not chaotic, choose no more than three types of plants, and plant them in big blocks of color along the bed.

Grow Up

Another way to use space is to plant tall, skinny plants that primarily grow up, not out. You can also make good use of space by planting climbing roses or vines. Make sure that you have a sturdy trellis firmly screwed into the wall for the plants to scramble up. Tie the plants to the trellis as they grow.

Just Grow With It!

Make vines do double duty in the garden by growing them like trees. In the left side of this picture, you can see a big pink bougainvillea vine growing up a trellis anchored to the wall. The vine remains fairly flat against the wall until it is about four to five feet off the ground. Once the vines reach the top of the wall, they're allowed to grow and flower, approximating the top of a tree. This is one way to add height to narrow gardens without the large root systems of trees. Coral honeysuckle vines are also good candidates for this type of growing and trellising.

Use Containers

If there's no room for plants in the ground in your narrow gardening space, place long, narrow containers along the fences or walls and plant those. You can plant shrubs, trees, vines with trellises, annuals, and perennials in containers to create gardens where there's little space or no soil.

One way to elevate containers to different heights is to use wrought-iron plant stands. The wrought iron is relatively thin and doesn't take up a lot of visual space. These plant stands can place plants at different heights along a wall or fence.

You can also hang hanging baskets all the way along an overhang bordering a narrow garden area. For a neat, orderly design, use hanging baskets made from the same materials with the same plant combinations. The key with narrow spaces is to be creative, and think up!

How to Plant a Container Garden

To really have fun in your garden, plant container gardens. You can find thousands of choices for pots at home-improvement stores and garden centers. If you look around your garage, you'll find interesting containers there too. Make sure that the container you select has drainage holes so that you don't drown your plants. Here's how to plant a container garden.

What You'll Need

- [ ] Potting soil (not garden soil)
- [ ] Flower pot or container
- [ ] Plants
- [ ] Watering can

Instant Green Thumb

Some plants are just made for container gardens. They spill gracefully over the edges of pots to soften the look of the containers. Here are your best bets for trailing plants:

- Scaevola
- Ivy
- Licorice plant
- Creeping jenny
- Verbena
- Calibrachoa
- Sweet potato vine

Step-by-Step

1 Select your plants. Container gardens need three types of plants: thrillers, fillers, and spillers. The pink SunPatien® in this group is the thriller, a stand-out plant. White angelonia is the filler, planted in odd numbers. Purple scaevola and chartreuse sweet potato vine are the spillers in this container.

2 Fill your container halfway with potting soil. (The bag will be marked "potting soil.") After you have the container half-full, you can begin placing your plants. Some plants will have larger rootballs than others, so you might should place the largest plant first then add additional soil to the container and place additional plants.

Just Grow With It!

Container gardens are great places to try new plants and interesting color combinations because if you don't like your creations, you can easily replant them. Here's a trick for creating container gardens that look like they were designed by a professional: make the plants "talk to each other." What does that mean? In such a small space, if you choose plants with six different colors, you'll have an eye-popping garden of color, and there's nothing wrong with that. If you select a group of plants in which each plant has at least one color in its leaves or flowers that is the same as another plant in the grouping, the overall effect is much more harmonious. In this picture, you can see the plants "talking." Burgundy/red, light green/chartreuse, and dark green are the three colors that are repeated in different ways in each of the plants. Isn't it lovely?

3 Finish placing your plants and add more soil to fill in the spaces between them. It's important that the plant stems aren't buried in soil so they don't rot. That's why you need to be careful when placing plants in the pots and place larger plants first. Don't be afraid to really pack the container full of plants. Because you usually grow them for only one season, their spacing doesn't matter as much.

4 Push the soil down at the edge of the container so that it is at least one inch below the edge of the pot. This leaves room for water to sit and soak in when you water the plant. If you fill the soil to the top of the container, it will all run out when you water the pot and will make a big mess. This is also a good time to sprinkle some slow-release fertilizer into the pot. Add it around the edges and on top of the soil—don't sprinkle it on top of the plants.

5 When you've finished planting, water the container. Give it a good soaking and let the water run out the bottom of the container. Then, wait several days to water again. A good rule of thumb is to water containers when the soil down to the second knuckle on your index finger (if you stick your finger in the pot) is dry. You should also water if the plants look droopy or saggy. Once the plants have grown to fill the pot, you'll need to water once or twice a day.

Success Tip

Plant a true container "garden" by planting small trees and shrubs in some containers and annuals or perennials in others. Try something new with large tropical plants like palms or bird of paradise as part of your plant combination. Group these plants in different-sized containers on a patio or walkway. You'll have an interesting movable garden that mimics the larger landscape.

Just Grow With It!

Myth: You should put gravel or broken pot shards in the bottom of your container to promote drainage.

Fact: Don't do this! You actually disrupt water flow in the pot if you change the materials halfway down the container. It's better to install a false bottom for your pot. These look like big plastic plates that fit halfway down in your pot to hold the soil and plants up, and you can find them at garden centers and home-improvement stores.

Tip: One way to make it easier to water container gardens is by starting with self-watering containers, which have water reservoirs at the bottom of the pots. A wicking system brings water to the plants. African violet pots are small self-watering containers, but now you can buy big landscape-sized containers too.

What to Plant in Your Container

Colorful annual flowers are a sure bet for containers, but you can also grow vegetables, herbs, perennials, and trees in pots.

Herb garden: You can grow all of your kitchen herbs in two pots. In one pot, plant basil and mint together. They both like to be slightly moist. In the other pot, plant oregano, sage, thyme, and rosemary together. Let that pot dry out before watering.

Salad bowl: Plant salad greens, bunching onions, and even radishes in a large, shallow dish. You can "cut and come again" to your salad bowl for weeks as salad greens keep producing leaves.

Perennial garden in a pot: Create containers that last from season to season by planting a small tree or shrub surrounded by perennials.

Herbs   *Perennials + Tree*   *Salad garden*   *Perennials*

How to Care for a Container Garden

One of the best reasons to plant container gardens is that it is easy to care for them. In a few minutes a week, you can keep your garden looking gorgeous. A few times a year, you can add new plants or move your container gardens to get more out of them. Think of them as "mobile mini gardens" that you can move around, and don't limit them to one season of show. Here's how to keep your container gardens looking great all year long.

What You'll Need

- ☐ Liquid fertilizer
- ☐ Watering can
- ☐ Hand pruners
- ☐ Bucket
- ☐ Evergreen plants

Instant Green Thumb

Container gardens generally stay pretty pest-free, but you will run into slug problems occasionally.

Slugs slime along your plants and munch holes in the leaves. Get rid of slugs by sprinkling some diatomaceous earth or crushed eggshells in your container close to the rim of the container. You can also make a beer trap with an old jar lid and cheap beer. Set that on the ground near your container, because slugs love beer and will fall into the trap and drown.

Container Care Techniques

Watering

To see if your container plants need water, stick your index finger in the pot. If the soil is dry down to your second knuckle of your index finger, water the pot.

Fertilizing

If you planted your container garden with potting mix that has slow-release fertilizer in it, you won't have to fertilize for a couple of months. After that, you'll need to fertilize containers with liquid fertilizer every three weeks. Read the package directions for mixing concentrated fertilizer with water.

Keeping Container Gardens Pretty All Year

Part of container garden care is renewing and refreshing. Sure, you can dump your garden in the fall and haul the plants to the compost bin, but you can also replant part or all of each container. To take a container from summer to winter, plant a small tree or shrub with evergreen leaves or interesting branch structure and color while you're planting during the spring.

You can then just replace the smaller surrounding plants at the beginning of each season, adding pansies for fall, winter, and spring, perennials for summer and winter, and bulbs for spring. Once the tree or shrub grows too large for the container, you can plant it outside in the garden.

Think outside the box when selecting container plants. Creating an interesting container garden means moving past petunias and pansies and putting something unexpected in your plant combination.

Camellia, coral bells, and violas

Red twig dogwood, holly, and black mondo grass

Deadheading

To keep your container gardens looking clean, remove the deadheads, or faded flowers. Some plant stems are soft enough that you can pinch off the dead flowers with your fingers. Others require pruning shears. Where you cut depends on the flower.

Some plants flower at the top of long stems. Once the flower is done blooming, nothing else will grow along the stem. In that case, cut the stem all the way back to the leaves at the base of the stem. Other flowers will resprout from along the stem. You can tell if that's the case by looking for a leaf with a tiny swelling or bud between the leaf and the stem. If that's the case, just remove the flower and part of the stem by cutting back to the bud.

Trees and Shrubs for Container Gardens

- Dwarf spruce
- Camellia
- Red and yellow twig dogwoods
- Golden mop Japanese falsecypress

- Boxwood
- Italian cypress
- 'Firepower' nandina
- 'Sky Pencil' holly

Success Tip

Containers are easy to care for in part because they're small (in comparison to a large garden). Plants in containers, however, are confined to growing in that small space, and are entirely dependent on the food and water you give them. As the plants grow, the roots take up more of the pot, and there's less room for water. Once your plants have grown and doubled in size, keep an eye on the water situation. If the plants dry out, you will have to water the containers twice a day.

Hardy succulents can stay outside - hens and chickens

Just Grow With It!

Zonal Denial

Because containers are portable, you can grow plants that need to be moved indoors in the winter. While you can grow many of these plants inside year-round, plants that prefer to be outside should be left outside as much as possible. Air conditioning and central heating make indoor air dry, which isn't ideal for most plants. Here's what to grow as part of your movable garden.

Citrus

Anyone can grow oranges, lemons, and limes in a pot. They need warm weather and full sun to flower and fruit. Plant them in individual pots, and place them as part of a larger container garden grouping. Bring them indoors during the winter and keep them beside a sunny windowsill.

Succulents

There are plenty of hardy succulents that withstand winter temperatures. Most hens and chickens (*Sempervivum* spp.) are cold-tolerant. If you just have to have a succulent container planted with flashy tender specimens, have no fear; bring it inside in the winter.

Tropical Plants

Most houseplants are tropical plants that naturally grow outdoors in Florida, Mexico, and Central or South America. Houseplants adore spending the summer outside, so use them to add some greenery to your garden of containers. Most houseplants need shade when they're outdoors.

Success Tip

Choose the right container for the right plants. Succulents don't need a lot of water, which means they don't need deep soil to grow. Plant succulent gardens in wide, shallow dishes. Clay pots dry out fast, so don't plant water hogs (like mint) in clay pots. Go for plastic instead.

Frost-tender succulents

Tropical plants

How to Select and Care for Houseplants

A house is not a home without plants. People naturally feel better and healthier when there's something green around them. Luckily, there are plenty of easy-to-grow houseplants, so you're sure to find one for that spot in the living room that needs a finishing touch. In addition to adding warmth and life to rooms, houseplants are fun to propagate and multiply, giving gardeners something to do while the snow flies outside. Here's how to select and grow houseplants.

What You'll Need

- ☐ Watering can
- ☐ Fertilizer
- ☐ Damp cloth
- ☐ Gravel
- ☐ Sticky traps
- ☐ Plant saucers
- ☐ Rooting powder
- ☐ Sharp knife

Instant Green Thumb

Many people overwater their houseplants. One rule of thumb for watering is this: the thicker the leaves, the less water the plant needs. Houseplants with thick leaves (including succulents, such as jade plants), need less water than plants with thin leaves (peace lilies).

Conversely, the thinner the leaf, the more water the plant will need.

How to Care for Houseplants

Elevate Humidity

Houseplants struggle with dry indoor air. Help them by adding a layer of gravel to the plant saucer and filling it with water so the water level covers the gravel by three-fourths. You don't want the pot sitting in water; you want the water to evaporate up around the plant leaves to raise humidity.

Water Plants Correctly

If your plants look saggy or droopy, they need water. You can also stick your finger in the pot. If the soil is dry down to the second knuckle on your index finger, it's time to water.

Just Grow With It!

Houseplants add as much to a room as other décor. With this in mind, plant your houseplants in interesting containers.

When planting in containers that don't have drainage holes, add a one-inch layer of gravel or decorative stones to the bottom of the pot. That creates a place for water to drain away from the plant root systems.

Create terrariums with your houseplants by planting them in glass containers with or without lids. Place a one-inch layer of gravel in the bottom of the container and add one-fourth inch of activated charcoal, which you find at pet supply stores. Top with soil, plant the plants, add water until the soil is damp, and cover. Enjoy your mini-greenhouse.

Control Houseplant Pests

The most common houseplant pests are scale, whiteflies, and fungus gnats. To control scale, you need to use a systemic insecticide, which is an insecticide that you water into the soil so that the plant can take it up. The insect will eat the plant and die. To catch whiteflies and other flying insects, use sticky traps, small pieces of paper that are coated with a sticky substance. Fungus gnats are problems for houseplants with soil that's too wet. Let the soil dry out and the gnats will go away.

Fertilize Houseplants

Plants growing outside constantly receive minerals and nutrients from the soil around them. Houseplants are confined to containers and get nothing other than what you provide for them. Houseplants don't need a lot of food, but they do benefit from fertilizer every few months. Use houseplant fertilizer according to label directions (adding it to the watering can), or water your houseplants with compost tea.

Water African Violets

African violets are picky about having water on their leaves. They like to have consistently moist, but not soaking wet, soil. Grow African violets in special pots. The bottom container is a non-porous bowl. That is where you put the water. The top container where you plant the violet is made of porous material or has wicking material to draw water from the bottom container into the soil. Just keep the bottom container filled with water, and you never have to guess when to water.

Fertilize African Violets

Easily feed African violets by adding fertilizer to the water in the self-watering container. Follow the instructions on the fertilizer label when adding fertilizer to make sure that you don't add too much.

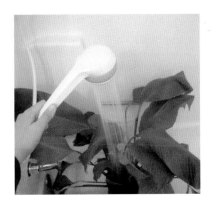

Give Houseplants a Shower

An easy way to clean houseplants that have been inside for a year is to put them in the shower. Let the water run over all of the plant leaves, into the pot, and down the drain. Soaking the plants like this washes out any fertilizer salts that may have built up in the pots. Let the plants drip dry, then move them back to their regular locations. They'll be as good as new.

The Best Houseplants For …

People who forget to water:

If you forget to water your houseplants for weeks at a time, buy a jade plant. These succulents can go without water for a month, and they'll be fine.

People who like to fuss with their plants:

If you like to care for your plants—cleaning, watering, turning, and snipping—get a peace lily. Peace lilies are easy to grow, but they also tolerate a high level of care. You can't kill these plants with kindness.

People who want low-maintenance but pretty houseplants:

The "duct tape" of houseplants is the golden pothos. It needs medium light and medium water, but will grow well under fluorescent lights, can be trimmed if it grows out of bounds, and will bounce back if it doesn't get enough water for a week or so.

Rubber plant   *Ivy*   *Bird's nest fern*

How to Select Houseplants

Light is the most important factor to consider when selecting houseplants. A pretty plant placed in an area with too much or not enough light will decline rapidly. The leaves will turn yellow and fall off, the stems will weaken and flop, and the plant won't grow. Before purchasing houseplants, figure out what type of light naturally falls in the area for which you need a plant. Then, use this list to go shopping.

Low Light

(Placed near an east- or north-facing window.)

- Golden pothos
- Peace lily
- Snake plant
- Schefflera
- Lady palm
- Dracaena

Medium Light

(Placed just out of direct sunlight—near a west- or south-facing window.)

- African violet
- Bird's nest fern
- Alocasia
- Ivy
- Spider plant

Bright Light

(Placed right next to a west- or south-facing window.)

- Palm
- Croton
- Bromeliad
- Cactus
- Rubber plant
- Ficus tree

Wipe Off Plant Leaves

Plants breathe and "eat" through their leaves. If the leaves are covered with dust and dirt, it's difficult for the plants to exchange carbon dioxide for oxygen. Dirt also keeps sunlight from reaching the leaves, and sunlight is one of the "ingredients" plants use to make food. Every couple of months, use a damp cloth to gently remove dust and dirt from houseplant leaves.

Peace lily   *Alocasia*   *Snake plant*   *Croton*

How to Propagate Houseplants

Propagating houseplants (growing new plants from the plants you already have) is a fun way to share plants with friends and add more plants to your house. If you want to start new spider plants, just snip the "baby" plants that grow off the big plants and put them in water so the hard, green roots of the babies are completely covered. To propagate golden pothos, cut off a six-inch piece of stem, remove the leaves from the bottom half of the stem, and put the bottom half in water. African violets are fun to propagate too. Follow these steps.

1 Use a sharp knife to cut off a leaf from the plant. You need at least one to two inches of "leaf stem." (The leaf stem is called the petiole. It connects the wide part of the leaf to the rest of the plant.)

2 Dip the leaf stem in rooting powder, which you can find at home-improvement stores and garden centers. Rooting powder is made from a natural plant hormone that stimulates root growth. You can propagate African violets without rooting powder, but they'll start growing faster with it.

3 Stick the stem in moist soil. Keep the soil watered and let the leaves sit for several weeks. Eventually, you'll start to see new, tiny leaves sprout from the base of the leaf that you cut off the old plant. Once the new plant has three leaves, you can gently transplant the plants into individual pots.

Glossary

4 tine claw

Also called a cultivator, this hand tool typically has 3 to 4 curved tines and is used to break up soil clods or lumps before planting and to rake soil amendments into garden beds.

Acidic soil

On the soil pH scale of 0–14, acidic soil has a pH lower than 6.5. Most garden plants prefer a soil a bit on the acidic side.

Afternoon sun

A garden receiving afternoon sun typically has full sun from 1 to 5 p.m. daily, with more shade during the morning hours.

Alkaline soil

On the soil pH scale from 0–14, alkaline soil has a pH higher than 6.5. Many desert plants thrive in slightly alkaline soils.

Annual

A plant that germinates (sprouts), flowers, and dies within one year or season (spring, summer, winter, or fall).

B&B (balled and burlapped)

Plants that have been grown in field nursery rows, dug up with their soil intact, wrapped with burlap, and are tied with twine. Most of the plants sold as B&B are large evergreen plants and deciduous trees.

Bareroot

Bareroot plants are those that are shipped dormant, without being planted in soil or having soil around their roots. Roses are often shipped bareroot.

Beneficial insect

Insects that perform valuable services such as pollination and pest control. Ladybugs, soldier beetles, and some bees are examples.

Biennial

A plant that blooms during its second year and then dies.

Blower

Blowers are garden tools that propel air out of a nozzle in order to remove leaves or other garden debris for easy clean-up. Electric, gas, and cordless models are available.

Bolting

When a plant switches from leaf growth to producing flowers and seeds. Bolting often occurs quite suddenly and is usually undesirable, because the plant usually dies shortly after bolting.

Brown materials

A part of a well-balanced compost pile, brown materials include high-carbon materials such as brown leaves and grass, woody plant stems, dryer lint, and sawdust.

Bt

Bacillus thuringiensis (Bt) is an organic pest control based on naturally occurring soil bacteria, often used to control harmful bugs like cutworms, leafrollers, and webworms.

Bud

An undeveloped shoot nestled between the leaf and the stem that will eventually produce a flower or plant branch.

Bulb

Plants with a large, rounded underground storage organ formed by the plant stem and leaves, such as tulips, daffodils, and hyacinths. Bulbs that flower in the spring are typically planted in the fall.

Bush

See *shrub*.

Common name

Common names are the names that are generally used to identify plants in different regions, as opposed to their scientific or horticultural names, which are standard throughout the world. For example, the common name for *Echinacea purpurea* is "purple coneflower."

Contact herbicide

These herbicides kill only the part of the plant that they touch, such as the leaves or the stems.

Container

Any pot or vessel that is used for planting. Containers can be ceramic, clay, steel, or plastic—or a teacup, bucket, or barrel.

Container garden

A garden that is created primarily by growing plants in containers instead of in the ground.

Cool-season annual

Flowers that thrive during cooler months, such as cyclamen, snapdragons, and pansies.

Cool-season vegetable

Vegetables that thrive during the cooler months, such as spinach, broccoli, and peas.

Cover crop

Plants that are grown specifically to enrich the soil, prevent erosion, suppress weeds, and control pests and diseases.

Dappled shade

Bright shade created by high tree branches or tree foliage, where patches of sunlight and shade intermingle.

Deadhead

The practice of consistently removing dead flowers in order to encourage further bloom, and to prevent the plant from going to seed.

Deciduous plant

Plants that lose their leaves seasonally, typically in the fall or early winter.

Diatomaceous earth

A natural control for snails, slugs, flea beetles, and other garden pests. It consists of the crushed fossilized remains of sea creatures.

Dibber

A tool consisting of a pointed wooden stick with a handle. Used for poking holes in the ground so seedlings, seeds, and small bulbs can be planted.

Divide

A technique consisting of digging up clumping perennials, separating the roots, and replanting. Dividing plants encourages vigorous growth and is typically performed in the spring or fall.

Dormant

The period when plants stop growing in order to conserve energy. This happens naturally and seasonally, usually in the winter.

Dripline

The ground area under the outer circumference of tree branches. This is where most roots draw water up into the tree.

Drop spreader

A garden tool that evenly distributes seed and herbicides. Particularly good for use near flower beds, because one piece of the spreader prevents the seed and fertilizer from going where you don't want it.

Dwarf

Plants with slow growing habits. Dwarf plants stay smaller, longer, but they can still grow to be quite large.

Evergreen

Plants that keep their leaves year-round, rather than dropping them seasonally.

Flower stalk

The stem that supports the flower and elevates it for insects to reach the flower and pollinate it.

Four-inch pot

The 4-inch by 4-inch pots that many annuals and small perennials are sold in. Four-inch pots can also be sold in flats of 18 or 20.

Frost

Ice crystals that form when the temperature falls below freezing (32 degrees F).

Full sun

Areas of the garden that receive direct sunlight 6 to 8 hours a day or more, with no shade.

Fungicide

A chemical compound used to destroy or control fungi or fungal spores.

Gallon container

A standard nursery-sized container for plants, roughly equivalent to a gallon container of milk.

Garden fork

A garden implement with a long handle and short tines used for loosening and turning soil.

Garden lime

A soil amendent that lowers soil acidity and raises the pH.

Garden soil

The existing soil in a garden bed; it is generally evaluated by its nutrient content and texture. Garden soil is also sold as a bagged item at garden centers and home-improvement stores.

Germinate

The process by which a plant emerges from a seed or a spore.

Granular fertilizer

Fertilizer that comes in a dry pellet-like form, rather than a liquid or powder.

Grass clippings

The parts of grass that are removed when mowing. Clippings are a valuable source of Nitrogen for the lawn or the compost pile.

Green materials

An essential element in composting that includes grass clippings, kitchen scraps, and manure, and provides valuable Nitrogen in the pile. Green materials are high in Nitrogen.

Hand pruners

An important hand tool that consists of two sharp blades that perform a scissoring motion. Used for light pruning, clipping, and cutting.

Hardening off

The process of slowly acclimating seedlings and young plants from an indoor growing environment to the outdoors.

Hardiness zone map

The hardiness zone map lists average annual minimum temperature ranges of a particular area, helpful in determining appropriate plants for the garden. North America is divided into 11 separate hardiness zones.

Hard rake

A tool with a long handle and rigid tines at the bottom. Great for moving a variety of garden debris such as soil, mulch, leaves, and pebbles.

Hedging

The practice of trimming a line of plants to create a solid mass for privacy or garden definition.

Heirloom

A plant that was more commonly grown during earlier periods of human history, but is not widely used in modern commercial agriculture.

Hoe

A long-handled garden tool with a short, narrow, flat steel blade. Used for breaking up hard soil and removing weeds.

Hose breaker

A device that screws onto the end of a garden hose to disperse the flow of water pressure from the hose.

Host plant

A plant grown to feed caterpillars that will eventually morph into butterflies.

Hybrid

A plant that is produced by crossing two genetically different plants. Hybrids often have desirable characteristics such as disease resistance.

Irrigation

A system of watering the landscape. Irrigation can be an in-ground automatic system, soaker or drip hoses, or hand-held hoses with nozzles.

Jute twine

A natural-fiber twine used for gently staking plants or tying them to plant supports.

Kneeling pad

A padded, weather-resistant cushion used for protecting knees while performing garden tasks such as weeding and planting.

Landscape fabric

A synthetic material that is laid on the soil surface to control weeds and prevent erosion.

Leaf rake

A long-handled rake with flexible tines on the head, used for easily and efficiently raking leaves into piles.

Liquid fertilizer

Plant fertilizer in a liquid form, may be either mixed with water or ready to use from the bottle.

Loppers

One of the largest types of the manual gardening tools, used for pruning branches between one to three inches in diameter using a scissoring motion.

Morning sun

Areas of the garden that have an eastern exposure and receive direct sun in the morning hours.

Mulch

Any type of material that is spread over the soil surface around the base of plants to suppress weeds and retain soil moisture.

Naturalized

Plants that are introduced into an area, as opposed to being native to it, are said to be naturalized.

Nectar plant

Flowers that produce nectar that attract and feed butterflies, encouraging a succession of blooms throughout the season.

New wood (new growth)

The new growth on plants that is characterized by a greener, more tender form than older, woodier growth.

Nozzle

A device that attaches to the end of a hose and disperses water through a number of small holes. The resulting spray covers a wider area.

Organic

Products derived from naturally occurring materials instead of materials synthesized in a lab.

Part shade

Areas of the garden that receive from 3 to 6 hours of sun a day. Plants requiring part shade will often require protection from the more intense afternoon sun, either from tree leaves or from a building.

Part sun

Areas of the garden that receive from 3 to 6 hours of sun a day. Although often interchangably used with "part shade," a part sun designation places greater emphasis on the minimal sun requirements.

Perennial

Plants that live for more than two years, including trees, shrubs, and flowering plants.

Pesticide

A substance used for destroying or controlling insects that are harmful to plants. Pesticides are available in organic and synthetic forms.

pH

A figure designating the acidity or the alkalinity of garden soil. pH is measured on a scale of 1–14, with 7.0 being neutral.

Pinch

Removing unwanted plant growth with your fingers, promoting bushier growth and increased blooming.

Pitchfork

A hand tool with a long handle and sharp metal prongs, typically used for moving loose material such as mulch or hay.

Plant label

The label or sticker on a plant container that provides information on plant description, care, and growth habits.

Pollination

The transfer of pollen for fertilization from one plant to another, usually by wind, bees, butterflies, moths, or hummingbirds. Required for fruit production.

Potting soil

A mixture used to grow flowers, herbs, and vegetables in containers, providing proper drainage and extra nutrients for healthy growth.

Powdery mildew

A fungal disease characterized by white powdery spots on plant leaves and stems, typically caused by water stress and poor air circulation.

Power edger

An electric or gasoline-powered edger that removes grass along flower beds and walkways for a neat appearance.

Pre-emergent herbicide

A weed killer that works by preventing weed seeds from sprouting.

Pruning

A garden task that uses a variety of hand tools to remove dead or overgrown branches to increase plant fullness and health.

Pruning saw

A hand tool for pruning smaller branches and limbs, featuring a long, serrated blade with an elongated handle.

Push mower

A lawn mower that is propelled by the user rather than a motor, typically having between 5 to 8 steel blades that turn and cut as the mower is pushed.

Reel mower

A mower in which the blades spin vertically with a scissoring motion to cut grass blades.

Rhizome

An underground horizontal stem that grows side shoots.

Riding mower

A rear engine lawn mower upon which the operator rides, perfect for mowing large areas more efficiently.

Rootball

The network of roots and soil clinging to a plant when it is lifted out of the ground.

Rotary spreader

A garden tool that distributes seed and herbicides in a pattern wider than the base of the spreader.

Scientific name

A two-word identifcation system consisting of the genus and species of a plant, such as *Ilex opaca*.

Scissors

A two-bladed hand tool great for cutting cloth, paper, twine, and other lightweight materials.

Seed packet

The package in which vegetable and flower seeds are sold, typically including growing instructions, planting charts, and harvesting information.

Seed starting mix

Typically a soilless blend of perlite, vermiculite, peat moss, and other ingredients specifically for growing plants from seed.

Shade

Garden shade is the absence of any direct sunlight in a given area, usually due to tree foliage or building shadows.

Shop broom

A long-handled broom with a wide base used for efficiently sweeping a variety of fine to medium debris.

Shovel

A handled tool with a broad, flat blade and slightly upturned sides for moving soil and other garden materials.

Shredded hardwood mulch

A mulch consisting of shredded wood that interlocks, resisting wash-out and suppressing weeds.

Shrub

A woody plant that is distinguished from a tree by its multiple trunks and branches, and shorter height of under 15 feet tall.

Shrub rake

A long-handled rake with a narrow head that fits easily into tight spaces between plants.

Side dress

Adding granular fertilizer or plant tone along the top of the soil to the side of the plant.

Slow-release fertilizer

A form of fertilizer that releases nutrients at a slower rate throughout the season, requiring less frequent applications.

Snips

A hand tool used for snipping small plants and flowers, perfect for harvesting fruits, vegetables, and flowers.

Soaker hose

An efficient watering system that typically uses recycled rubber to produce porous hoses that allow water to seep out around plant roots.

Soil knife

A garden knife with a sharp, serrated edge for cutting twine, plant roots, turf, and other garden materials.

Soil test

An analysis of a soil sample that determines the level of nutrients (to identify deficiencies) and detects any existing contaminants.

Spade

A short-handled tool with a sharp, rectangular metal blade that cuts and digs soil or turf.

String trimmer

A hand-held tool that uses monofilament line instead of a blade to trim grass.

Succulent

A type of plant that stores water in its leaves, stems, and roots and is acclimated for arid climates and soil conditions.

Sucker

The odd growth from the base of a tree or a woody plant, often caused by stress. Also refers to sprouts from below the graft of a rose or fruit tree. Suckers divert energy away from the desirable tree growth and should be removed.

Summer annual

Annuals that thrive during the warmer months of the growing season.

Systemic herbicide

A weed killer that is absorbed by the plant's roots or foliage that destroys all parts of the plant.

Taproot

An enlarged, tapered plant root that grows vertically downward.

Transplants

Plants that are grown in one location and then moved to and planted in another. Seeds started indoors and nursery plants are two examples.

Tree

A woody perennial plant that typically consists of a single trunk with multiple lateral branches.

Tree canopy

The upper layer of growth consisting of the tree's branches and leaves.

Tropical plant

Plants that are native to the tropical regions of the world, acclimated to warm and humid climates.

Trowel

A hand tool that is used for digging or moving around small amounts of soil.

Turf

Grass and the surface layer of soil that is held together by its roots.

Variegated

The appearance of differently colored areas on plant leaves, usually white, yellow, or a brighter green.

Vegetable

A plant or part of a plant that is used for food.

Warm-season vegetable

Vegetables that thrive during the warmer months, such as tomatoes, okra, and peppers.

Watering wand

A hose attachment that features a longer handle for watering plants beyond your reach.

Weed and feed

A product containing both an herbicide for weed control and a fertilizer for grass growth.

Weeping

A growth habit in plants that features drooping or downward curving branches.

Wheat straw

The dry stalks of wheat that are used for mulch, retaining soil moisture, and suppressing weeds.

Wood chips

Small pieces of wood made by cutting or chipping, and used as mulch in the garden.

Featured Plant Information

The plants featured in this book are listed in this chart, which notes annuals, perennials, bulbs, trees, and shrubs in alphabetical order according to the names (usually common names) used in the book. Look at the key to understand their light and water needs.

FS=Full Sun
PS=Part Sun
S=Shade

L=Water less than once a week
M=Water weekly or when the soil is dry
H=Needs consistently moist soil

Common name	Scientific name	Plant type	Zone	Light	Water
Ageratum	*Ageratum houstonianum*	Annual	—	FS	M
Ajuga	*Ajuga reptans*	Perennial	4-8	PS	M
Allium	*Allium* spp.	Bulb	3-9	FS	L
Alyssum	*Lobularia maritima*	Annual	—	FS	M
Amsonia	*Amsonia tabernaemontana*	Perennial	3-9	FS-PS-S	M
Anemone	*Anemone coronaria*	Bulb	6-9	PS	M
Angelonia	*Angelonia angustifolia*	Annual	—	FS-PS	M
Anise hyssop	*Agastache foeniculum*	Perennial	5-9	FS-PS	L
Annual salvia	*Salvia* spp.	Annual	—	FS	L
Arborvitae	*Thuja occidentalis*	Tree or shrub	2-7	FS-PS	M
Artemisia	*Artemisia schmidtiana*	Perennial	3-7	FS-PS	L
Asiatic lily	*Lilium* spp.	Bulb	4-8	FS	L
Aspen	*Populus tremuloides*	Tree	1-6	FS	M
Astilbe	*Astilbe* x *arendsii*	Perennial	4-9	S	M
Atlas cedar	*Cedrus atlantica*	Tree	6-9	FS	L
Azalea	*Rhododendron* hybrids	Shrub	6-9	PS-S	M
Bald cypress	*Taxodium distichum*	Tree	4-9	FS	H
Balloon flower	*Platycodon grandiflorus*	Perennial	3-8	FS-PS	M
Bearded iris	*Iris germanica*	Perennial	3-9	S	L
Beautyberry	*Callicarpa americana*	Shrub	6-10	FS-PS	M
Bee balm	*Monarda* spp.	Perennial	3-7	FS	M
Beech	*Fagus grandifolia*	Tree	3-9	FS	L
Begonia	*Begonia* spp.	Annual	10-11	S	L

Common name	Scientific name	Plant type	Zone	Light	Water
Black-eyed Susan	*Rudbeckia* spp.	Perennial	3-9	FS-PS	M
Blackgum	*Nyssa sylvatica*	Tree	3-9	FS	L
Black mondo grass	*Ophiopogon* 'Nigrescens'	Perennial	6-9	FS-PS-S	L
Blazing star	*Liatris* spp.	Perennial	3-8	FS	L
Bleeding heart	*Dicentra* spp.	Perennial	3-9	S	H
Blue spruce	*Picea pungens*	Tree	2-7	FS	L
Bluebeard	*Caryopteris incana*	Shrub	5-9	FS-PS	M
Borage	*Borago officinalis*	Herb	—	FS-PS	M
Bottlebrush buckeye	*Aesculus parviflora*	Shrub	4-8	FS-PS	M
Boxwood	*Buxus* spp.	Shrub	4-9	PS	L
Burr oak	*Quercus macrocarpa*	Tree	3-8	FS	L
Calendula	*Calendula officinalis*	Annual	—	FS	L
Calibrachoa	*Calibrachoa* hybrids	Annual	—	FS	M
California poppy	*Eschscholzia californica*	Annual	—	FS	L
Camellia	*Camellia* spp.	Tree	8-10	S	L
Candytuft	*Iberis sempervirens*	Perennial	3-8	PS-S	M
Canna	*Canna* hybrids	Bulb	7-10	FS	H
Cardinal flower	*Lobelia cardinalis*	Perennial	3-9	FS	H
Carolina silverbell	*Halesia carolina*	Tree	4-8	FS-PS	M
Celosia	*Celosia* spp.	Annual	—	FS	M
Chamomile	*Chamaemelum nobilis*	Herb	4-9	FS	L
Cherry	*Prunus* spp.	Tree	5-8	FS	L
Chinese fringe tree	*Chionanthus retusus*	Tree	5-9	PS	M
Chives	*Allium schoenoprasum*	Herb	4-8	FS	L
Chrysanthemum	*Chrysanthemum*	Perennial	5-9	FS	M
Coffee berry	*Rhamnus californica*	Shrub	7-9	FS	L
Coleus	*Solenostemon* spp.	Annual	—	PS-S	M
Columbine	*Aquilegia* x *hybrida*	Perennial	4-7	PS-S	M
Coneflower	*Echinacea purpurea*	Perennial	3-8	FS	L
Coral bells	*Heuchera* spp.	Perennial	4-9	PS-S	L
Cosmos	*Cosmos* spp.	Annual	—	FS	M
Cotoneaster	*Cotoneaster horizontalis*	Shrub	5-7	FS-PS-S	L

Common name	Scientific name	Plant type	Zone	Light	Water
Crabapple	*Malus* spp.	Tree	5-8	FS	L
Crape myrtle	*Lagerstroemia indica*	Tree	6-9	FS-PS	L
Creeping jenny	*Lysimachia nummularia*	Perennial	3-9	FS-PS-S	L
Creeping phlox	*Phlox stolonifera*	Perennial	5-9	FS-PS	L
Crocosmia	*Crocosmia* spp.	Bulb	6-9	FS-PS	L
Cryptomeria	*Cryptomeria japonica*	Tree	5-9	PS	L
Daffodil	*Narcissus* hybrids	Bulb	4-8	FS-PS	L
Dahlia	*Dahlia* hybrids	Bulb	7-10	FS	M
Dawn redwood	*Metasequoia glyptostroboides*	Tree	4-8	FS	M
Daylily	*Hemerocallis* hybrids	Perennial	3-9	FS-PS	L
Diamond frost	*Euphorbia* 'Diamond Frost'	Annual	10-12	FS	L
Dianthus	*Dianthus* spp.	Annual or perennial	6-8	FS-PS	M
Dill	*Anethum graveolens*	Herb	—	FS	M
Douglas fir	*Pseudotsuga menziesii*	Tree	4-6	FS	L
Dusty miller	*Senecio cineraria*	Annual	—	FS-PS	L
Elephant ear	*Colocasia esculenta*	Bulb	8-10	FS-PS	H
Epimedium	*Epimedium* spp.	Perennial	5-9	PS-S	M
Eupatorium	*Eupatorium* spp.	Perennial	5-9	FS	M
Falsecypress	*Chamaecyparis pisifera*	Shrub or tree	4-8	FS	L
False indigo	*Baptisia alba*	Perennial	5-8	FS-PS	M
Fennel	*Foeniculum vulgare*	Herb	4-9	FS-PS	M
Firethorn	*Pyracantha angustifolia*	Shrub	5-9	FS-PS	L
Flowering dogwood	*Cornus florida*	Tree	5-9	FS-PS-S	L
Flowering kale	*Brassica oleracea*	Annual	—	FS-PS	M
Flowering plum	*Prunus* spp.	Tree	5-7	FS	L
Flowering tobacco	*Nicotiana alata*	Annual	—	FS	M
Foamflower	*Tiarella cordifolia*	Perennial	4-9	PS-S	L
Forget-me-not	*Myosotis sylvatica*	Perennial	3-8	PS-S	M
Giant rudbeckia	*Rudbeckia maxima*	Perennial	5-8	FS	L
Ginger lily	*Alpinia japonica*	Perennial/ bulb	8-11	FS-PS	H
Gladiola	*Gladiolus* hybrids	Bulb	—	FS	L
Goatsbeard	*Aruncus dioicus*	Perennial	3-7	PS-S	M

Common name	Scientific name	Plant type	Zone	Light	Water
Golden mop Japanese falsecypress	*Chamaecyparis pisifera* 'Golden Mop'	Shrub	5-7	FS	L
Golden raintree	*Koelreuteria paniculata*	Tree	5-9	FS	L
Gooseneck loosestrife	*Lysimachia clethroides*	Perennial	3-8	FS-PS	M
Green ash	*Fraxinus pennsylvanica*	Tree	3-9	FS	L
Gaura	*Gaura lindheimeri*	Perennial	5-9	FS	L
Hardy ice plant	*Delosperma cooperi*	Perennial	5-11	FS	L
Hawthorn	*Crataegus* spp.	Tree	4-7	FS	L
Sneezeweed	*Helenium* spp.	Perennial	4-8	FS	M
False sunflower	*Heliopsis helianthoides*	Perennial	3-9	FS	M
Hens and chickens	*Sempervivum*	Perennial	4-10	FS	L
Highbush cranberry	*Viburnum trilobum*	Shrub	2-7	PS	M
Hornbeam	*Carpinus caroliniana*	Tree	3-9	FS	L
Hosta	*Hosta*	Perennial	3-8	PS-S	L
Hydrangea	*Hydrangea* spp.	Shrub	Varies	PS-S	M
Impatiens	*Impatiens walleriana*	Annual	—	S	M
Japanese painted fern	*Athyrium niponicum* 'Pictum'	Perennial	4-8	S	L
Joe Pye weed	*Eutrochium purpureum*	Perennial	3-9	FS	L
Katsura	*Cercidiphyllum japonicum*	Tree	4-8	FS	L
Korean spice viburnum	*Viburnun carlesii*	Shrub	4-8	PS-S	L
Kousa dogwood	*Cornus kousa*	Tree	5-8	FS-S	L
Lady's mantle	*Alchemilla mollis*	Perennial	3-8	FS-PS	M
Lamb's ear	*Stachys byzantina*	Perennial	4-10	PS	L
Lantana	*Lantana* 'New Gold'	Perennial	7-11	FS	L
Larkspur	*Delphinium consolida*	Annual	—	FS-PS	M
Lavender	*Lavandula angustifolia*	Perennial/ herb	5-8	FS	L
Lenten rose	*Helleborus* spp.	Perennial	5-8	PS	M
Leopard plant	*Ligularia* spp.	Perennial	3-8	PS-S	M
Licorice plant	*Helichrysum petiolare*	Annual	—	FS	L
Lily of the Nile	*Agapanthus* spp.	Bulb	6-10	FS-PS	L
Lily of the valley	*Convallaria majalis*	Perennial/ bulb	3-8	S	H
Lilyturf	*Lirope* spp.	Perennial	4-10	FS-PS-S	L
Little bluestem	*Schizachyrium scoparium*	Ornamental grass	3-9	FS	L

Common name	Scientific name	Plant type	Zone	Light	Water
Little gem magnolia	*Magnolia grandiflora* 'Little Gem'	Tree	7-9	FS	L
Loropetalum	*Loropetalum chinense*	Shrub	7-10	FS-PS-S	L
Louisiana iris	*Iris* spp.	Perennial/bulb	5-9	PS	H
Lungwort	*Pulmonaria*	Perennial	4-9	PS-S	M
Magnolia	*Magnolia* spp.	Tree	4-8	FS	L
Marigold	*Tagetes* spp.	Annual	—	FS	L
Marjoram	*Origanum*	Herb	6-9	FS	L
Melampodium	*Melampodium divaricatum*	Annual	—	FS	M
Meserve holly	*Ilex* x *meserve*	Shrub	4-7	FS	L
Mexican hat	*Ratibida columnifera*	Perennial	4-9	FS	H
Mexican sage	*Salvia leucantha*	Perennial	8-10	FS	L
Milkweed	*Asclepias* spp.	Perennial	3-9	FS-PS	M
Mimosa	*Albizia julibrissin*	Tree	6-9	FS	M
Mint	*Mentha* spp.	Herb/perennial	3-11	FS-PS-S	H
Miscanthus	*Miscanthus* spp.	Ornamental grass	5-9	FS	L
Firepower nandina	*Nandina domestica* 'Firepower'	Shrub	6-11	FS-PS	L
Nasturtium	*Trapaeolum* spp.	Annual	—	FS	M
Native American plum	*Prunus americana*	Tree	3-8	FS	L
New England aster	*Symphyotrichum novae-angliae*	Perennial	4-8	FS	M
Oregano	*Origanum vulgare*	Herb	5-10	FS	L
Ornamental cabbage	*Brassica oleracea*	Annual	—	FS	M
Osteospermum	*Osteospermum*	Annual	—	FS	M
Japanese pachysandra	*Pachysandra terminalis*	Perennial	5-9	PS-S	M
Pansy	*Viola* x *wittrockiana*	Annual	—	FS-PS	M
Paperbark maple	*Acer griseum*	Tree	4-8	FS-PS	M
Paper birch	*Betula papyrifera*	Tree	2-6	FS-PS	M
Parsley	*Petroselinum crispum*	Herb	—	FS-PS	M
Pawpaw	*Asimina triloba*	Tree	5-9	FS	M
Penstemon	*Penstemon* spp.	Perennial	3-8	FS	L
Peony	*Paeonia lactiflora*	Perennial	3-8	PS	M
Periwinkle	*Catharanthus roseus*	Annual	—	FS	M
Persian shield	*Strobilanthes dyerianus*	Annual	—	S	M

Common name	Scientific name	Plant type	Zone	Light	Water
Petunia	*Petunia* hybrids	Annual	—	FS	M
Phlox	*Phlox paniculata*	Perennial	4-8	FS-PS	M
Pieris	*Pieris japonica*	Shrub	5-8	PS-S	L
Pincushion flower	*Scabiosa* spp.	Perennial	4-8	FS	M
Pine	*Pinus* spp.	Tree	3-8	FS	L
Podocarpus	*Podocarpus machrophyllus*	Tree	7-9	FS-PS	M
Polka dot plant	*Hypoestes phyllostachya*	Annual	—	PS-S	M
Portulaca	*Portulaca grandiflora*	Annual	—	FS	L
Potentilla	*Potentilla*	Shrub	4-7	FS	L
Primrose	*Primula*	Annual	—	FS-PS	M
Princess tree	*Paulowinia tomentosa*	Tree	5-8	FS	L
Purple coneflower	*Echinacea purpurea*	Perennial	3-8	FS	L
Red maple	*Acer rubrum*	Tree	3-9	FS	L
Red oak	*Quercus rubra*	Tree	4-8	FS	L
Red twig dogwood	*Cornus sericea, C. alba*	Shrub	3-7	FS-PS	M
Redbud	*Cercis canadensis*	Tree	4-8	FS-PS-S	M
Rhododendron	*Rhododendron* spp.	Shrub	4-8	PS-S	M
River birch	*Betula nigra*	Tree	4-9	FS	H
Rosemary	*Rosmarinus officinalis*	Herb	8-10	FS	L
Rudbeckia	*Rudbeckia* cvs.	Annual or perennial	—	FS	L
Russian sage	*Perovskia atriplicifolia*	Perennial	5-9	FS	L
Scaevola	*Scaevola*	Annual	—	FS-PS	M
Scotch pine	*Pinus sylvestris*	Tree	2-7	FS	L
Sea thrift	*Armeria maritima*	Perennial	4-8	FS	L
Sedum	*Sedum* spp	Perennial	3-9	FS	L
Serviceberry	*Amelanchier* spp.	Tree	2-8	FS-PS	M
Shrub rose	*Rosa* spp.	Shrub	3-8	FS	L
Siberian bugloss	*Brunnera macrophylla*	Perennial	3-8	PS-S	M
Sky pencil holly	*Ilex crenata* 'Sky Sentry'™	Shrub	5-9	FS	L
Skyrocket juniper	*Juniperus scopulorum* 'Skyrocket'	Shrub	4-9	FS	L
Smoketree	*Cotinus* spp.	Tree	4-8	FS	L
Smooth sumac	*Rhus glabra*	Shrub	3-9	FS	L

Common name	Scientific name	Plant type	Zone	Light	Water
Snapdragon	*Antirrhinum majus*	Annual	—	FS	M
Solomon's seal	*Polygonatum biflorum*	Perennial	3-8	S	M
Sorrel	*Rumex acetosa*	Herb	3-7	FS	L
Southern magnolia	*Magnolia grandiflora*	Tree	7-9	FS	L
Spanish bluebell	*Hyacinthoides hispanica*	Bulb	3-8	FS-PS-S	L
Spiderwort	*Tradescantia* spp.	Perennial	4-7	PS-S	H
Spruce	*Picea* spp.	Tree	2-7	FS	L
Star magnolia	*Magnolia stellata*	Tree	4-8	FS	L
Stock	*Matthiola incana*	Annual	—	FS-PS	M
Sugar maple	*Acer saccharum*	Tree	3-8	FS	L
Sunflower	*Helianthus annuus*	Annual	—	FS	L
SunPatien®	*Impatiens*	Annual	—	FS-PS	M
Swamp hibiscus	*Hibiscus coccineus*	Perennial/ shrub	6-9	FS-PS	H
Swamp sunflower	*Helianthus angustifolia*	Perennial	6-9	FS-PS	H
Sweet gum	*Liquidambar styraciflua*	Tree	5-9	FS	M
Sweet pea	*Lathyrus odoratus*	Annual	—	FS-PS	L
Sweet potato vine	*Ipomoea batatas*	Annual	—	FS-PS	L
Sweet William	*Dianthus barbatus*	Biennial	3-9	FS-PS	M
Sweet woodruff	*Galium ordoratum*	Perennial	4-8	PS	M
Swiss chard	*Beta vulgaris*	Annual	—	FS-PS	M
Switchgrass	*Panicum virgatum*	Ornamental grass	5-9	FS	L
Sycamore	*Platanus occidentalis*	Tree	4-9	FS	L
Tea olive	*Osmanthus fragrans*	Shrub	9-11	FS-PS	L
Thyme	*Thymus* spp.	Herb	4-9	FS	L
Toad lily	*Tricyrtis* spp.	Perennial	5-8	PS-S	H
Torenia	*Torenia fournieri*	Annual	—	FS-S	M
Tree lilac	*Syringa reticulata*	Tree	3-7	FS	L
Tulip	*Tulipa* hybrids	Bulb	3-8	FS	L
Tulip poplar	*Liriodendron tulipifera*	Tree	4-9	FS	L
Turtlehead	*Chelone glabra*	Perennial	3-8	PS-S	M
Umbrella plant	*Cyperus alternifolius*	Annual	—	FS	H
Verbena	*Verbena* spp.	Annual/perennial	varies	FS	L

Common name	Scientific name	Plant type	Zone	Light	Water
Viola	*Viola* spp.	Annual	—	FS-PS	M
Virginia bluebells	*Mertensia virginica*	Bulb	3-8	PS-S	M
Virginia sweetspire	*Itea virginica*	Shrub	5-9	FS-PS	H
Weeping beech	*Fagus sylvatica* 'Pendula'	Tree	4-7	FS	L
Weeping cherry	*Prunus* spp.	Tree	5-8	FS	M
Weigela	*Weigela florida*	Shrub	4-8	FS-PS	M
Western red cedar	*Thuja plicata*	Tree	5-7	FS	L
White fir	*Abies concolor*	Tree	3-7	FS	L
Winterberry holly	*Ilex verticillata*	Shrub	3-9	FS-PS	L
Yarrow	*Achillea* spp.	Perennial	3-8	FS	L
Yucca	*Yucca filamentosa*	Perennial	5-10	FS	L
Zelkova	*Zelkova serrata*	Tree	5-8	FS	L
Zinnia	*Zinnia* spp.	Annual	—	FS	M

Index

African violet
    fertilizing, 170
    watering, 170

annuals
    care, 102–103
    cool-weather, 99
    planting, 98
    purchasing, 38
    selection, 98–101
    warm-weather
        shade, 101
        sun, 100

aphids, 148

bagworms, 95

blackspot, 94

blossom end rot, 146

botrytis (gray mold), 131

broadleaf weed killer, 35

broad-spectrum weed killer, 35

brown materials, 61
    see also compost

brown patch, 74

bulbs, flowering, 124–29

butterflies, attracting, 119

cabbage white butterfly, 149

cedar apple rust, 95

chipmunks, 149

compost
    how to, 60
    ingredients, 61
    problems, 61

container gardens
    care, 164

    deadheading, 166
    fertilizing, 164
    planting, 160–63, 167
    trees and shrubs, 166
    watering, 164

containers
    in narrow spaces, 159
    purchasing, 39

deadheading
    annuals, 102
    container gardens, 166
    perennials, 111

decomposition, see compost

deer, 95, 130

diatomaceous earth, 34, 131, 149

double digging, 117

drought, 146

edging (landscape beds), 152

evergreens, 83

fairy ring, 74

fertilizer, 29–30
    label, reading, 50–51
    organic, 51
    purchasing, 40
    slow-release, 51
    synthetic, 51

fertilizing
    annuals, 103
    container gardens, 164

flowering plants
    annuals
        care, 102–103

Photo Credits

These photos © copyright to photographers listed below.

Tom MacCubbin
Brown patch P. 74

Yvonne Cunnington
Serviceberry flowers (left) P. 84, Serviceberry P. 85

Jo Ellen Meyers Sharp
Serviceberry flower (right) P. 84

Tina Koral
Serviceberry fruit (left) P. 84

Mary Ann Newcomer
Serviceberry fruit (right) P. 84

Istock
Cedar apple rust P. 95
Slug P. 149

Carol Bradford
Powdery mildew P. 131

Lee Reich
Blossom end rot P. 146

Daniel Gasteiger
Squash bugs P. 148

Barbara Wise
Perennials + tree P. 163
Perennials P. 163
Photos P. 165

Kathy Purdy
Botrytis P. 131

Bill Johnson
Bagworms P. 95
Deer P. 95
Aphids P. 148
Squash vine borer moth P. 148

Rebecca Sweet
Just Grow With It P. 159

Kylee Baumle
Japanese beetles P. 131
Tomato hornworm Pgs. 132, 149
Cabbage white butterfly P. 149
Chipmunk P. 149

All plant closeups are by Katie Elzer-Peters © unless otherwise indicated on this list.

Meet Katie Elzer-Peters

Katie Elzer-Peters has been gardening since she could walk, a hobby—turned career—nurtured by her parents and grandparents. After receiving a Bachelor of Science in Public Horticulture from Purdue University, Katie completed the Longwood Graduate Program at Longwood Gardens and the University of Delaware, receiving a Master of Science in Public Garden Management.

Katie has served as a horticulturist, head of gardens, educational programs director, development officer, and manager of botanical gardens around the United States, including the Washington Park Arboretum in Seattle, Washington; the Indianapolis Zoo in Indianapolis, Indiana; the Marie Selby Botanical Garden in Sarasota, Florida; the Smithsonian Institution in Washington, D.C.; Longwood Gardens in Kennett Square, Pennsylvania; Winterthur Museum, Garden and Library in Greenville, Delaware; The King's Garden at Fort Ticonderoga in Ticonderoga, New York; and Airlie Gardens in Wilmington, North Carolina.

Whether at a botanical garden or for a garden center, garden club, or school group, Katie has shared her love of gardening by teaching classes and workshops, and writing brochures, articles, gardening content, and columns. While serving as Curator of Landscape at Fort Ticonderoga, Katie planned and led garden bus tours along the East Coast of the United States and Canada.

Today, Katie lives and gardens with her husband and dog in the coastal city of Wilmington, North Carolina, (zone 7b). She *loves* the year-round weather for gardening, but is in constant battle with the sandy soil. Katie manages GreatGardenSpeakers.com, an online speaker directory of garden, design, ecology, and horticultural speakers. She also owns The Garden of Words, LLC, a marketing and PR firm specializing in garden-industry clients.

Beginner's Illustrated Guide to Gardening is her first book for Cool Springs Press.